Bola Agbaje

Gone Too Far!

Methuen Drama

Published by Methuen Drama 2007

Methuen Drama, an imprint of Bloomsbury Publishing Plc

3 5 7 9 10 8 6 4

Methuen Drama
Bloomsbury Publishing Plc
50 Bedford Square
London WC1B 3DP
www.methuendrama.com

ISBN: 978 0 713 68698 2

A CIP catalogue record for this book is available from the British Library

Available in the USA from Bloomsbury Academic & Professional,
175 Fifth Avenue/3rd Floor, New York, NY 10010.
www.BloomsburyAcademicUSA.com

Typeset by Country Setting, Kingsdown, Kent
Printed and bound by
CPI Group (UK) Ltd, Croydon, CR0 4YY

ROYAL COURT

Royal Court Theatre presents

GONE TOO FAR!

by **Bola Agbaje**

First performance at the Royal Court Jerwood Theatre Upstairs,
Sloane Square, London on 2nd February 2007.

The Young Writers Festival is supported by
John Lyon's Charity
Columbia Foundation
The Foyle Foundation

GONE TOO FAR!

by **Bola Agbaje**

Armani **Zawe Ashton**
Yemi **Tobi Bakare**
Old Lady **Maria Charles**
Razer **Ashley Chin**
Policeman 2 **Phillip Edgerley**
Shop Keeper/Policeman 1 **Munir Khairdin**
Ikudayisi **Tunji Lucas**
Flamer **Ricci McLeod**
Mum/Paris **Bunmi Mojekwu**
Blazer **Marcus Onilude**

Director **Bijan Sheibani**
Designer **James Cotterill**
Lighting Designer **Nicki Brown**
Sound Designer **Emma Laxton**
Choreographer **Aline David**
Assistant Director **Laura McCluskey**
Casting **Amy Ball**
Production Manager **Sue Bird**
Stage Managers **Carla Archer, Shianne McFarlane**
Costume Supervisor **Jackie Orton**

THE COMPANY

Bola Agbaje (writer)
Bola was part of the Critical Mass Writers'
Group in January 2006. This is her first play.

Zawe Ashton
Theatre includes: Teddy Girls, The Big Nickel
(Soho); A Midsummer Night's Dream, Old Vic
Gala (National Youth Theatre).
Television includes: Mobile, The Crust, Holby
City, East Enders, NCS Manhunt, In Deep,
The Bill, Wild House, Demon Headmaster,
Game On.
Film includes: Spiralling, Shooters.

Tobi Bakare
Theatre includes: Macbeth (Out of Joint); Totally
Over You, Mr Yama Yama, Romeo and Juliet
(Arcola).
Film includes: Bad Mouth, Ugly.
Tobi is currently training at Identity Drama
School.

Nicki Brown (lighting designer)
For the Royal Court: 93.2FM (& UK tour).
Other theatre includes: The Elephant Man (UK
and Brazilian tour); Hamlet (UK and Beirut);
By Parties Unknown (Sincera Productions);
Splendour, Dr Faustus (Etcetera).
Nicki is lighting assistant at the Royal Court.

Maria Charles
Theatre includes: The Boyfriend, Divorce Me
Darling, The Matchmaker, Annie, Steaming,
Fiddler on the Roof, Hay Fever, Follies (West
End); Tartuffe (tour); Good Person of Sezchuan,
Absence of War, The Wind in the Willows
(National); School for Scandal (Theatre Clwyd);
Blithe Spirit (Basingstoke); Driving Miss Daisy
(Salisbury Playhouse); Measure for Measure
(Riverside Studios); Lower Depths (Foco Novo);
The Yiddish Trojan Women (Cockpit); Richard III
(Stafford Festival).
Television includes: Barmitzvah Boy, Sheppey,
Holby City, Down to Earth, Secret Army, Agony
Again, Coronation Street, Bad Girls III,
Brideshead Revisited, Never the Twain, Agony,
Oliver Twist, Crime and Punishment.
Film includes: Hott Fuzz, 66, Derailed, Great
Expectations, Revenge of the Pink Panther,
Victor/Victoria.

Ashley Chin
For the Royal Court: Lift Off.
Film includes: Storm Damage.

James Cotterill (designer)
Theatre includes: Big Sale (The Place); Fair
(Trafalgar Studios); Silverland, 15 Minutes
(Arcola); Widows, The Fool (RADA);
The Gabriel's (Finborough).
Awards include: 2005 Linbury Prize for stage
design for Not the End of the World (Bristol
Old Vic).

Aline David (choreographer)
Theatre includes: Swan Lake (Ballet of Rhin);
Cendrillon of Massenet, La Grande Duchesse of
Gerolstein d'Offenbach, L'Italiana in Algeria of
Rossini, L'Africaine de Meyerbeer, The Tempest
(Rhin National Opera); Le Barbier de Seville of
Rossini (Palais des Congres et de la Musique de
Strasbourg); The Queen of Spades (Royal Opera
House); The Tempest (Royal Opera House,
London and Copenhagen).

Phillip Edgerley
Theatre includes: Julius Caesar (Lyric
Hammersmith); Two Gentlemen of Verona, Julius
Caesar (RSC); Duck Variations, Kiss of the
Spiderwoman, Mary Stuart, Hamlet (Nuffield);
Much Ado About Nothing, Dr Faustus (Oxford
Shakespeare Co.); Luther (National); On the
Razzle (Chichester Festival Theatre); A Bedfull of
Foreigners (New Theatre Royal, Portsmouth);
Dancing at Lughnasa, Been So Long (Jermyn
Street); Another Country (Brockley Jack);
Bookworms, The Crucible, King Lear (Fringe).
Television and film includes: Footballers' Wives,
Extra Time, Dead Rich, Ultimate Force, Life As
We Know It, East Enders, The Bill, Chicane.
Radio includes: Bernice Sommerfield,
Doctor Who.

Munir Khairdin
Theatre includes: Foxes (West Yorkshire
Playhouse); The Hot Zone, (Lyric
Hammersmith); Calcutta Kosher (Kali Theatre
Co.); Behzti (Birmingham Rep.); Bombay Dreams
(Apollo Victoria); Romeo & Juliet (Hazlitt Open
Air); Rashomon, Butcher's Skin (Yellow Earth);
The Trial, Merchant of Venice (Cherub Co.);
Romeo & Juliet (Leicester Haymarket).
Film and television includes: Britz, Rendition, It
Was an Accident, Spooks.

Emma Laxton (sound designer)
For the Royal Court: Catch, Scenes from the
Back of Beyond, Woman and Scarecrow, The
World's Biggest Diamond, Incomplete and

Random Acts of Kindness, My Name Is Rachel Corrie (also West End/Galway Festival/Edinburgh Festival/Minetta Lane, New York), Bone, The Weather, Bear Hug, Terrorism, Food Chain.
Other theatre includes: Other Hands (Soho); The Unthinkable (Sheffield); My Dad is a Birdman (Young Vic); The Gods Are Not to Blame (Arcola); Late Fragment (Tristan Bates). Emma is Sound Deputy at the Royal Court.

Tunji Lucas
Theatre includes: The Small Things (Menier Chocolate Factory).

Ricci McLeod
For the Royal Court: Catch.
Other theatre includes: Two Step (Almeida); Zonal (Lyric Hammersmith); Burning Ambitions (Riverside Studios).
Television includes: The Bill, Dub Plate Drama, Ghost Squad, Casualty, William & Mary (series 1, 2 & 3), Doctors, Green Wing.
Film includes: Football Factory.

Bunmi Mojekwu
Theatre includes: Totally Over You (Arcola). Bunmi is currently training at Identity Drama School.

Marcus Onilude
Theatre includes: Arthur (Arcola); Unknown Child, In the Mind (Anna Scher Festival). Marcus is currently training at Identity Drama School.

Bijan Sheibani (director)
As director, theatre includes: Fixer (Almeida); Other Hands, Flush (Soho); Breath, Party Time/One for the Road (BAC); Have I None (Southwark Playhouse); Summer (Lion and Unicorn); Nightwatchman (Oval Cricket Ground); Peace for our Time (Cockpit); The Lover (Burton Taylor).
As assistant director for the Royal Court: Terrorism.
As assistant director, other theatre includes: The Tempest (Royal Opera House); Cinderella (China Children's National Theatre); As You Like It (Wyndham's); A Dream Play (National); Primo (National Theatre Studio); Twelfth Night (English Touring Co.); The Io Passion (Aldeburgh/Almeida/Bregenz).

ROYAL COURT BAR & FOOD

MONDAY TO SATURDAY 11AM - 11PM
RESERVATIONS
020 7565 5058

THE ENGLISH STAGE COMPANY
AT THE ROYAL COURT

The English Stage Company at the Royal Court opened in 1956 as a subsidised theatre producing new British plays, international plays and some classical revivals.

The first artistic director George Devine aimed to create a writers' theatre, 'a place where the dramatist is acknowledged as the fundamental creative force in the theatre and where the play is more important than the actors, the director, the designer'. The urgent need was to find a contemporary style in which the play, the acting, direction and design are all combined. He believed that 'the battle will be a long one to continue to create the right conditions for writers to work in'.

Devine aimed to discover 'hard-hitting, uncompromising writers whose plays are stimulating, provocative and exciting'. The Royal Court production of John Osborne's Look Back in Anger in May 1956 is now seen as the decisive starting point of modern British drama and the policy created a new generation of British playwrights. The first wave included John Osborne, Arnold Wesker, John Arden, Ann Jellicoe, N F Simpson and Edward Bond. Early seasons included new international plays by Bertolt Brecht, Eugène Ionesco, Samuel Beckett and Jean-Paul Sartre.

The theatre started with the 400-seat proscenium arch Theatre Downstairs, and in 1969 opened a second theatre, the 60-seat studio Theatre Upstairs. Some productions transfer to the West End, such as Tom Stoppard's Rock 'n' Roll, My Name is Rachel Corrie, Terry Johnson's Hitchcock Blonde, Caryl Churchill's Far Away and Conor McPherson's The Weir. Recent touring productions include Sarah Kane's 4.48 Psychosis (US tour) and Ché Walker's Flesh Wound (Galway Arts Festival). The Royal Court also co-produces plays which transfer to the West End or tour internationally, such as Conor McPherson's Shining City (with Gate Theatre, Dublin), Sebastian Barry's The Steward of Christendom and Mark Ravenhill's Shopping and Fucking (with Out of Joint), Martin McDonagh's The Beauty Queen Of Leenane (with Druid), Ayub Khan Din's East is East (with Tamasha).

Since 1994 the Royal Court's artistic policy has again been vigorously directed to finding and producing a new generation of playwrights. The writers include Joe Penhall, Rebecca Prichard, Michael Wynne, Nick Grosso, Judy Upton,

photo: Stephen Cummiiskey

Meredith Oakes, Sarah Kane, Anthony Neilson, Judith Johnson, James Stock, Jez Butterworth, Marina Carr, Phyllis Nagy, Simon Block, Martin McDonagh, Mark Ravenhill, Ayub Khan Din, Tamantha Hammerschlag, Jess Walters, Ché Walker, Conor McPherson, Simon Stephens, Richard Bean, Roy Williams, Gary Mitchell, Mick Mahoney, Rebecca Gilman, Christopher Shinn, Kia Corthron, David Gieselmann, Marius von Mayenburg, David Eldridge, Leo Butler, Zinnie Harris, Grae Cleugh, Roland Schimmelpfennig, Chloe Moss, DeObia Oparei, Enda Walsh, Vassily Sigarev, the Presnyakov Brothers, Marcos Barbosa, Lucy Prebble, John Donnelly, Clare Pollard, Robin French, Elyzabeth Gregory Wilder, Rob Evans, Laura Wade, Debbie Tucker Green, Levi David Addai and Simon Farquhar. This expanded programme of new plays has been made possible through the support of A.S.K. Theater Projects and the Skirball Foundation, The Jerwood Charity, the American Friends of the Royal Court Theatre and (in 1994/5 and 1999) the National Theatre Studio.

The refurbished theatre in Sloane Square opened in February 2000, with a policy still inspired by the first artistic director George Devine. The Royal Court is an international theatre for new plays and new playwrights, and the work shapes contemporary drama in Britain and overseas.

The Royal Court's long and successful history of innovation has been built by generations of gifted and imaginative individuals. For information on the many exciting ways you can help support the theatre, please contact the Development Department on 020 7565 5079.

AWARDS FOR
THE ROYAL COURT

Marina McDonagh won the 1996 George Devine Award the 1996 Writers' Guild Best Fringe Play Award, the 1996 Critics' Circle Award and the 1996 Evening Standard Award for Most Promising Playwright for The Beauty Queen of Leenane. Marina Carr won the 19th Susan Smith Blackburn Prize (1996/7) for Portia Coughlan. Conor McPherson won the 1997 George Devine Award, the 1997 Critics' Circle Award and the 1997 Evening Standard Award for Most Promising Playwright for The Weir. Ayub Khan Din won the 1997 Writers' Guild Awards for Best West End Play and New Writer of the Year and the 1996 John Whiting Award for East is East (co-production with Tamasha).

Martin McDonagh's The Beauty Queen of Leenane (co-production with Druid Theatre Company) won four 1998 Tony Awards including Garry Hynes for Best Director. Eugene Ionesco's The Chairs (co-production with Theatre de Complicite) was nominated for six Tony awards. David Hare won the 1998 Time Out Live Award for Outstanding Achievement and six awards in New York including the Drama League, Drama Desk and New York Critics Circle Award for Via Dolorosa. Sarah Kane won the 1998 Arts Foundation Fellowship in Playwriting. Rebecca Prichard won the 1998 Critics' Circle Award for Most Promising Playwright for Yard Gal (co-production with Clean Break).

Conor McPherson won the 1999 Olivier Award for Best New Play for The Weir. The Royal Court won the 1999 ITI Award for Excellence in International Theatre. Sarah Kane's Cleansed was judged Best Foreign Language Play in 1999 by Theater Heute in Germany. Gary Mitchell won the 1999 Pearson Best Play Award for Trust. Rebecca Gilman was joint winner of the 1999 George Devine Award and won the 1999 Evening Standard Award for Most Promising Playwright for The Glory of Living.

In 1999, the Royal Court won the European theatre prize New Theatrical Realities, presented at Taormina Arte in Sicily, for its efforts in recent years in discovering and producing the work of young British dramatists.

Roy Williams and Gary Mitchell were joint winners of the George Devine Award 2000 for Most Promising Playwright for Lift Off and The Force of Change respectively. At the Barclays Theatre Awards 2000 presented by the TMA, Richard Wilson won the Best Director Award for David Gieselmann's Mr Kolpert and Jeremy Herbert won the Best Designer Award for Sarah Kane's 4.48 Psychosis. Gary Mitchell won the Evening Standard's Charles Wintour Award 2000 for Most Promising Playwright for The Force of Change. Stephen Jeffreys' I Just Stopped by to See the Man won an AT&T: On Stage Award 2000.

David Eldridge's Under the Blue Sky won the Time Out Live Award 2001 for Best New Play in the West End. Leo Butler won the George Devine Award 2001 for Most Promising Playwright for Redundant. Roy Williams won the Evening Standard's Charles Wintour Award 2001 for Most Promising Playwright for Clubland. Grae Cleugh won the 2001 Olivier Award for Most Promising Playwright for Fucking Games.

Richard Bean was joint winner of the George Devine Award 2002 for Most Promising Playwright for Under the Whaleback. Caryl Churchill won the 2002 Evening Standard Award for Best New Play for A Number. Vassily Sigarev won the 2002 Evening Standard Charles Wintour Award for Most Promising Playwright for Plasticine. Ian MacNeil won the 2002 Evening Standard Award for Best Design for A Number and Plasticine. Peter Gill won the 2002 Critics' Circle Award for Best New Play for The York Realist (English Touring Theatre). Ché Walker won the 2003 George Devine Award for Most Promising Playwright for Flesh Wound. Lucy Prebble won the 2003 Critics' Circle Award and the 2004 George Devine Award for Most Promising Playwright, and the TMA Theatre Award 2004 for Best New Play for The Sugar Syndrome. Richard Bean won the 2005 Critics' Circle Award for Best New Play for Harvest. Laura Wade won the 2005 Critics' Circle Award for Most Promising Playwright and the 2005 Pearson Best Play Award for Breathing Corpses. The 2006 Whatsonstage Theatregoers' Choice Award for Best New Play was won by My Name is Rachel Corrie. The 2005 Evening Standard Special Award was given to the Royal Court 'for making and changing theatrical history this last half century'.

Tom Stoppard's Rock 'n' Roll won the 2006 Evening Standard Award for Best Play.

ROYAL COURT BOOKSHOP

The Royal Court bookshop offers a range of contemporary plays and publications on the theory and practice of modern drama. The staff specialise in assisting with the selection of audition monologues and scenes. Royal Court playtexts from past and present productions cost £2.
The Bookshop is situated to the right of the stairs leading to the ROYAL COURT CAFE BAR.

Monday to Friday 3 – 10pm
Saturday 2.30 – 10pm
(Closed shortly every evening from 7.45 to 8.15pm)

For information tel: 020 7565 5024

or email: bookshop@royalcourttheatre.com

Books can also be ordered from our website www.royalcourttheatre.com

PROGRAMME SUPPORTERS

The Royal Court (English Stage Company Ltd) receives its principal funding from Arts Council England, London. It is also supported financially by a wide range of private companies, charitable and public bodies, and earns the remainder of its income from the box office and its own trading activities.

The Genesis Foundation supports the Royal Court's work with International Playwrights.

The Artistic Director's Chair is supported by a lead grant from The Peter Jay Sharp Foundation, contributing to the activities of the Artistic Director's office. Over the past nine years the BBC has supported the Gerald Chapman Fund for directors.

Archival recordings of the Royal Court's Anniversary year were made possible by Francis Finlay.

ROYAL COURT
SLOANE SQUARE

23 February – 10 March
Jerwood Theatre Upstairs

THE ELEVENTH CAPITAL

by **Alexandra Wood**

direction **Natalie Abrahami**

From rural backwater to shiny new capital city in one easy move. Perfectly formed. Politically constructed. When your leader plays pin the tail on the donkey with the nations map the bureaucrats are bound to be moved and everyone will follow. The Eleventh Capital is an arresting new play about dislocation, manipulation and power. You can't stop the march of progress, no one can.

Supported by John Lyon's Charity, Columbia Foundation, The Foyle Foundation.

18 January – 17 March
Jerwood Theatre Downstairs

THE SEAGULL

by **Anton Chekhov**
in a new version by
Christopher Hampton

direction **Ian Rickson**
design **Hildegard Bechtler**
lighting **Peter Mumford**
sound **Ian Dickinson**
music **Stephen Warbeck**
cast **Denise Black, Mackenzie Crook, Chiwetel Ejiofor, Paul Jesson, Art Malik, Carey Mulligan, Christopher Patrick Nolan, Katherine Parkinson, Pearce Quigley, Mary Rose, Kristin Scott Thomas, Peter Wight**

"Now I understand, Kostya, I've understood, that with our work – it doesn't matter whether it's acting or writing – what's essential is not fame or success, none of the things I used to dream about: it's about the ability to endure."

THE SEAGULL is one of the great plays about writing. It superbly captures the struggle for new forms, the frustrations and fulfilments of putting words on a page. Chekhov, in his first major play, stages a vital argument about the theatre which still resonates today.

Supported by an anonymous donor and the Laura Pels Foundation.

BOX OFFICE 020 7565 5000
BOOK ONLINE
www.royalcourttheatre.com

FOR THE ROYAL COURT

Artistic Director **Dominic Cooke**
Associate Director International **Elyse Dodgson**
Associate Directors **Ramin Gray, Emily McLaughlin,
Sacha Wares**
Associate Director Casting **Lisa Makin**
Literary Manager **Graham Whybrow**
Literary Associate **Terry Johnson***
Casting Deputy **Amy Ball**
International Administrator **Chris James**
Trainee Director **Lyndsey Turner**
Artistic Assistant **Rebecca Hanna-Grindall**

Production Manager **Paul Handley**
Deputy Production Manager **Sue Bird**
Production Assistant **Sarah Davies**
Head of Lighting **Johanna Town**
Lighting Deputy **Greg Gould**
Lighting Assistants **Nicki Brown, Kelli Marston**
Lighting Board Operator **Stephen Andrews**
Head of Stage **Steven Stickler**
Stage Deputy **Daniel Lockett**
Stage Chargehand **Lee Crimmen**
Head of Sound **Ian Dickinson**
Sound Deputy **Emma Laxton**
Acting Head of Costume **Jackie Orton**

YOUNG WRITERS PROGRAMME
Associate Director **Ola Animashawun**
Administrator **Nina Lyndon**
YWF Assistant Producer **Claire Birch***
Outreach Worker **Lucy Dunkerley**
Education Officer **Laura McCluskey***
Writers' Tutor **Leo Butler***

General Manager **Diane Borger**
Administrator **Oliver Rance**
Finance Director **Sarah Preece**
Acting Head of Finance **Helen Perryer**
Finance Officer **Rachel Harrison***
Finance Officer **Martin Wheeler**

Head of Communications **Kym Bartlett**
Advertising and Marketing Agency **aka**
Press Officer **Stephen Pidcock**
Marketing Assistant **Gemma Frayne**
Marketing Intern **Áine Mulkeen**
Press Intern **Nicole Slavin**

Sales Manager **David Kantounas**
Deputy Sales Manager **Stuart Grey**
Box Office Sales Assistants **Daniel Alicandro,
Helen Bennett, Annet Ferguson**

Head of Development **Nicky Jones**
Development Consultant (maternity cover)
Caroline Hawley
Trusts and Foundations Manager **Gaby Styles**
Sponsorship Officer **Natalie Moss**
Development Intern **Hannah Proctor**

Theatre Manager **Bobbie Stokes**
Front of House Managers **Nathalie Meghriche,
Lucinda Springett**
Bar and Food Manager **Darren Elliott**
Deputy Bar and Food Manager **Claire Simpson**
Duty House Managers **Charlie Revell***, **Matt Wood***
Bookshop Manager **Simon David**
Assistant Bookshop Manager **Edin Suljic***
Bookshop Assistants **Nicki Welburn***, **Fiona Clift***
Building Maintenance Administrator **Jon Hunter**
Stage Door/Reception **Simon David***,
Paul Lovegrove, Tyrone Lucas

Thanks to all of our box office assistants, ushers
and bar staff.

* Part-time.

ENGLISH STAGE COMPANY

President
Sir John Mortimer CBE QC

Vice President
Dame Joan Plowright CBE

Honorary Council
**Sir Richard Eyre CBE
Alan Grieve CBE
Martin Paisner CBE**

Council
Chairman **Anthony Burton**
Vice Chairwoman **Liz Calder**

Members
**Judy Daish
Graham Devlin
Sir David Green KCMG
Joyce Hytner OBE
Tamara Ingram
Stephen Jeffreys
Phyllida Lloyd
James Midgley
Sophie Okonedo
Katharine Viner**

Gone Too Far!

To my brother Ladi Agbaje who sometimes goes too far.
I hope you realise you can *turn back.*

I would like to thank God, who has answered my prayers
and guided me on the right path.

Mum, Dad, Bisola, Bisi, Biola, Wendy, Vivian, Sophie:
the best family a girl could ask for. Sharma, Beno, Nyah,
Simone, Esther and all those who have been a part of my life
one way or another: you have all played a role in shaping
who I am today. A big thank you to the Royal Court Theatre
and Bijan Sheibani for your time and effort on this play.

Characters

Yemi, *sixteen, black, stubborn, short-tempered, does not understand or speak Yoruba, good-looking*

Ikudayisi, *eighteen, black, has an African accent which he changes to a fake American one when he is around other people, apart from Yemi; he speaks Yoruba*

Mum, *has an African accent and speaks Yoruba*

Shopkeeper, *Muslim Bangladeshi with an accent, wears a headscarf*

Armani, *fifteen, mixed race, speaks fast, with an attitude*

Paris, *sixteen, dark-skinned, pretty, very calm, with a soft-spoken voice*

Old Lady, *old and frail*

Razer, *seventeen, good-looking, dresses well*

Flamer, *seventeen, light-skinned, good-looking, wears the latest fashion, everything brand new*

Blazer, *eighteen, black, tall, well built; his presence shows he is not someone to mess with*

Police Officers 1 *and* **2**, *white, cockney accents*

Scene One

It is mid-afternoon and we are in **Yemi***'s bedroom. It is a small room which is suitable for one but is clearly occupied by two. A single bed with a duvet cover on it and a mattress on the floor with only the sheets take up most of the space. There are suitcases on the floor, opened with clothes hanging out from them, a mixture of traditional African and casual attire. There is a small TV on the floor with a PS2 attached to it.*

Ikudayisi *is squatting up and down, pulling his ears. He is performing some sort of punishment; he has been doing it for a while and looks tired, but does not stop. He is wearing jeans and a T-shirt, which represent a fashion trend a few months behind the current times.* **Yemi***, on the other hand, is kneeling down on the floor playing on his PlayStation; he is better dressed than* **Ikudayisi** *and is up to fashion in the clothing department. He has on the latest hoodie and a fresh pair of white trainers. He does not pay any attention to* **Ikudayisi** *behind him, who tries to glance over his shoulder every time he squats.* **Yemi** *is engrossed in his game.*

Ikudayisi Can I play when you finish?

Yemi *does not respond.*

Ikudayisi Oh, don't go that way-oh!

Yemi *looks round and cuts his eye at him.*

Ikudayisi Is it games you are supposed to be doing or your punishment?

Yemi *remains silent.*

Ikudayisi It's not fair-oh!

Yemi *still remains silent and continues to focus on his games.*

Ikudayisi If you don't start doing your own I will tell Mum.

Yemi LEAVE ME!

Mum *shouts from offstage.*

Mum *(off)* Yemi. Is that your voice I'm hearing? Ahh ahh. Is that what I told you to be doing?

Yemi *jumps up from his game and begins his punishment.*

Yemi   It wasn't me, Mum!

Mum *(off)*   You better not be playing games up there. If I catch you . . . Ah! / You will not know yourself-oh!

Yemi   I'm not doing anything.

He starts to pack the games away quickly, and goes back to squatting like **Ikudayisi**. **Mum** *continues her rant from offstage; she is moving around so the volume goes up and down.*

Mum *(off)*   You these children, you these children, you are trying to kill me but I won't let you. Before I go from this earth I will show you pepper. People are always telling me I am lucky to have big boys like you. They don't know-oh, they don't know. You don't do nothing for me. You don't cook, you don't clean. All you do is give me problems. If I have to come up that stairs today . . .

The phone rings and she answers in a very English voice.

Hello. Oh yes, yes. Don't worry, I will be bringing it tomorrow . . .

Her voice trails off.

Yemi   You're such an idiot.

Ikudayisi   What level was you on?

Yemi   Don't talk to me, man.

Ikudayisi   Did you save it?

Yemi   Stop talking to me.

They continue their punishment in silent, **Yemi** *struggling more than* **Ikudayisi**.

Ikudayisi   Do you know the punishment you are doing, it is not the one she told you to do.

Yemi   Don't talk to me, man. Can't you just shut your mouth?

Mum *(off)*   Ah ah! Yemi, Oluyemi, is that you again. Do you want me to come up there today? If I have to walk up these stairs . . .

Yemi *moves to the floor to continue his punishment – left hand stretched out, with his right leg up in the air and his right hand behind his back.*

Mum *(off)*   . . . you will not like the side of me that you will see.

Yemi   It wasn't me, Mum, it was him that keeps on talking – he is tryna get me in trouble.

Ikudayisi   *Ma, mi o se nkon kon –* [Mum, I'm not doing anything –]

Mum *(off)*   IKUDAYISI!

Ikudayisi   Yes, Ma?

Mum *(off)*   *Wa bi baiyi.* [Come here.]

Ikudayisi   *Ma, mi o se nkon kon.* [Mum, I'm not doing anything.]

Mum *(off)*   *A bi ori ko pe ni?* [Is your head not correct?]

Ikudayisi   *Mon bo, Ma.* [I'm coming, Mum.]

Yemi   GOOD!

Ikudayisi *exits.*

Yemi *continues to do his punishment, but only for a little while. He looks at the door, waits for a sound and, when he does not hear anything, goes back to his computer game. As he is about to start playing,* **Mum** *calls him again.*

Mum *(off)*   YEMI OLUYEMI!

Yemi *jumps back to his punishment position.*

Yemi   Yes, Mum! Whatever he said he is lying. I'm still doing it. He is just tryna get me in trouble.

Mum *(off)*   Yemi, Yemi, I said come here.

Yemi   Mum, yeah, you told me do something, I'm doing it.

Mum *(off)*   Are you OK? Ah ah, nonsense. Is it me that you are talking to like dat? If I have to come up that stairs –

Yemi   AHHHH, MAN!

Yemi *leaves the room as* **Ikudayisi** *returns and barges into him on the way out.* **Mum** *is still ranting and raving.* **Ikudayisi** *picks up* **Yemi***'s computer game and starts playing.*

Mum (*off*)   – you have no respect. It not your fault, it not your fault. It's my own, I have spoilt you too much. When I should have taken you to Nigeria, to boarding school, I let you stay here and now look at you.

Yemi *and* **Mum** *continue their conversation offstage while* **Ikudayisi** *plays on the computer game, listening.*

Yemi   Yes, Mum.

Mum   You and your brother go to the shop for me.

Yemi   What? Why can't Dayisi go alone?

Mum   Don't start that nonsense with me. Don't start.

Yemi   But Mum, why don't he go?

Mum   He does not know de way.

Yemi   The shop is only round the corner.

Mum   You are going with your brother and that is final.

Yemi   But Mum, man!

Mum   Who are you calling man? Shut up, shut up your mouth. You listen up and you listen well. When I tell you to do something you do it. Don't ask me no silly questions. He is going to the shop with you and I don't want no trouble.

She shouts for **Ikudayisi***.*

Mum   Ikudayisi! Ikudayisi!

Ikudayisi   Ma?

Mum   *Mo fe ki ewo ati Yemi lo si shop fumi.* [I want you and Yemi to go to the shop for me.]

Ikudayisi   Yes, Ma.

He starts putting on his shoes, but then sees some Nike Air trainers in a box on **Yemi**'s *side of the room and picks them up. He puts on the trainers and start profiling in front of a mirror.*

Ikudayisi (*to himself*)   Hey, fine boy. Cool guy!

He does a bit of breakdancing. **Yemi** *and* **Mum** *continue to talk offstage.*

Yemi   MUM! I don't want him to go with me. I will go by myself.

Mum   Yemi, don't start-oh, don't start. Do you think I'm stupid, do you think I'm stupid? When I send you by yourself, you will just go and galavant on the street. I said he is going with you. He is going! Always you, always you, giving me problems. I'm too young to die-oh. You better go and buy me milk now, and you better come back quick quick.

Yemi   OK!

Mum   It is always you. Always you giving me high blood pressure. I will kill you before you kill me. I will kill you!

Yemi   OK, OK! I'm going.

Blackout.

Scene Two

Yemi *and* **Ikudayisi** *walk out onto the estate. It is run-down, with graffiti all over the walls. It is the scene of a typical south London estate with rows of flats. The shop is at the far end of the stage and the* **Shopkeeper** *is outside putting up a newspaper stand. There is Islamic music playing loudly from inside the shop and he is singing along to it. He is wearing an England shirt and a headscarf. There are also England flags hanging all around the shop. He immediately notices the boys and hovers around the door watching them closely.* **Yemi** *has his hood over his head.*

Ikudayisi   How much did she give you?

Yemi   Don't talk to me.

Ikudayisi   If there is money left I want to buy chocolate.

Yemi *ignores him and bops ahead towards the shop. As soon as they get to the door, the* **Shopkeeper** *stands in the way.* **Yemi** *tries to walk past him, but he refuses to move away from the door.*

Yemi   Scuse, boss.

The **Shopkeeper** *clears his throat and points to the hood.*

Shopkeeper   No hoods.

Yemi   Uhhh.

He attempts to get past again but fails.

Can you move out of the way?

Shopkeeper   Sorry, no hoods.

Yemi   I wanna buy something dough.

Shopkeeper   I said no hoods allowed.

Yemi   And who are you?

Shopkeeper   My shop, my rule.

Yemi   Come out the way, I need to buy somink.

Shopkeeper   Take off hood and you can enter.

Yemi   This ain't Tesco, you nah.

Ikudayisi   Yo bro, why don't you just take off the hood, man, it will save a lotta trouble.

Shopkeeper   Yes, listen to friend.

Yemi, *stunned by the accent, turns and looks at* **Ikudayisi**, *puzzled.*

Yemi (*to* **Shopkeeper**)   Be quiet. (*To* **Ikudayisi**.) What's with the accent?

Ikudayisi   What accent, man?

Yemi   That one! You need to lauw dat, man, cos it don't sound good. We're not in America, we're in England!

He looks down and sees his trainers on **Ikudayisi**.

Yemi   What are you doing with my trainers on?

Ikudayisi   I'm borrowing them. Don't you think it looks nice on me?

Yemi   No, it don't suit you.

Ikudayisi   You know I look fine, fine.

Yemi   Look, yeah, what have I told you bout taking my stuff?

Ikudayisi   What's your problem? You can have it back when we get home.

Yemi   Just *don't* touch my stuff. Goss, man, do I need to start putting a padlock on my shit?

Bored by the conversation, the **Shopkeeper** *starts to go inside, and* **Yemi** *tries to follow. The* **Shopkeeper** *puts his hand in* **Yemi**'s *face to stop him.*

Shopkeeper   Still have hood.

Yemi   I ain't ere to teef nothing. I just need to buy somink. So *move*, man!

Shopkeeper   I don't want trouble.

Yemi   And no one ain't looking for trouble, boss. Just let me in.

Shopkeeper   Please, I don't want to call police.

Yemi   What! You're making me mad now. Why are you talking bout police for? We only here to buy something, you get me?

Ikudayisi   He doesn't get you, he not moving.

Yemi   Shut up! I'm not talking to you! Just stand over there, man.

Ikudayisi *moves to the side and watches* **Yemi**.

Yemi   Boss, stop the long ting and let me in.

Shopkeeper   Take off hood.

Yemi   Just move!

Shopkeeper   Please, no trouble.

Yemi   Don't you know nothing about human rights? You of all people should understand where I'm coming from – being a Muslim and dat.

Shopkeeper   Are you Muslim?

Ikudayisi   No, he is not-oh.

Yemi (*to* **Ikudayisi**)   You eediate, I said no one ain't talking to you. Just be quiet. (*To* **Shopkeeper**.) No I'm not a Muslim. But you're Muslim, innit?

Shopkeeper   Yes.

Yemi   See, that's what I'm saying, we're the same peoples.

Shopkeeper   I no black, I Bangladeshi.

Yemi   I know you're Indian –

Shopkeeper   Bangladeshi.

Yemi   Don't get it twisted, blud. Man, oh man, don't care where you're from. What I'm saying is I *know* you feel oppressed and dat when mans tell you, you can't wear your head ting in certain places. It the same like me! Bare people going around thinking you're gonna do dem something when all *we* wanna do is get on with our life. I understand you, blud!

Shopkeeper   Then no hood.

Yemi   You're not getting what – Hold up. (*To* **Ikudayisi**.) Listen to the music this guy is tryna play.

Ikudayisi   It nice.

He mimics the song and tries to sing along.

Yemi   Shut up, man. It's not nice. (*To* **Shopkeeper**.) How do we know it isn't some Islamic chant that you're playing?

Shopkeeper   It's prayer music.

Yemi   You only saying that cos we don't understand it. Furthermore, how do I know it ain't a bomb factory you got back there? That why you ain't tryna let me in.

Shopkeeper   I NO BOMBER, I NO SUPPORT TERRORIST!

He moves towards **Yemi**, *waving his hands in his face.*

Shopkeeper   I LOVE THIS COUNTRY. I NO TERRORIST. NO BOMB IN MY SHOP, NO BOMB IN MY SHOP.

Yemi   Don't start coming nears me now, you might try blow me up –

Shopkeeper   You mutta mutta, you lie, no bomb in my shop –

Yemi   Look at the way you acting. You see, you see, that's why you of all people shouldn't judge, cos you're not liking it when you're getting judged.

Shopkeeper   I NO EVER SAY BAD THING ABOUT ENGLAND.

Yemi   Calm down, man, I was just making a point. Just cos I got a hood on my head don't mean I'm tryna rob nobody. Same ways *I know* just cos you're Indian don't mean you're a BOMBER!

Shopkeeper   I TELL YOU ALREADY I NO BOMBER! I PROUD TO BE ENGLISH. NO TROUBLE, NO TROUBLE. SHOP CLOSE, SHOP CLOSE.

The **Shopkeeper** *goes inside and closes the door.* **Yemi** *tries to open the door but it is locked.*

Yemi   Let me in! Don't you understand English? I was just making a point.

Shopkeeper (*from behind the door*)   Go away! I will call police now. You trouble.

Yemi *begins kicking on the door.*

Yemi   That's what I can't stand bout you Indians! Smelling of curry, coming over here, taking up all the corner shops, and man can't buy nothing. What da fuck you got a shop for if you're not tryna sell nothing? Call the police, call the police, I ain't doing nothing.

Ikudayisi   This is stupid, let's just go.

Yemi   I ain't going nowhere. Let the police come. (*To* **Shopkeeper**.) YOU HEAR ME? CALL THE POLICE. What can they do me for? It's more like they'll come and search up your shop. I just need to tell them you got a bomb in there. I bet *you* get arrested before I do!

The **Shopkeeper** *has now turned off his Islamic music and is playing the England World Cup song: 'Three Lions on the Shirt'.*

Ikudayisi   Let's just go, it not worth it at all, you are just scaring him.

Yemi   Scaring him? I should be scared of *him*. He is strange man!

Ikudayisi   It's not worth it.

Yemi   And what would you know? You wasn't even here on July the seventh when *his* people blew up bare heads last year.

Ikudayisi   What has that got to do with you wearing your hood in the shop? And you are lying – I heard about the July story. Not all Indian people are the same, and one of them was even black. Look at you, you should not judge like that.

Yemi   You're so backwards! Don't you know nothing at all? That how they look at us. Dem people are racist, they don't like black people, and I don't like dem either.

Ikudayisi   It's not cos you are black that he shut the door.

Yemi   You have a lot to learn.

Ikudayisi   I don't need to learn rubbish. You have to pick your battles well. Taking your hood off is nothing. You could have put it back on when we have finished.

Yemi   Shut up!

He pushes past **Ikudayisi** *and starts banging and kicking the door.*

Yemi   Let me in, you bloody Paki. You're going on like I ain't got money. I got bare dough.

Ikudayisi   He is not going to open de door when you are acting like a baboon.

Yemi *stops and turns to* **Ikudayisi***.*

Yemi   Baboon! You're one to talk. You da one who lived in da jungle.

Ikudayisi   Your head is not correct.

Yemi *tries to punch* **Ikudayisi** *but misses.*

Ikudayisi   You are foolish, you don't know yourself.

Yemi   You eediate, you so dumb. I wish you would just go back to where you belong. You get on my nerves.

Ikudayisi   I am here to stay so you better digest it well well.

Yemi   Why don't you just piss off and die?

Yemi *pushes* **Ikudayisi***, who falls to the ground.*

Ikudayisi   OK, I'll go home.

He turns to leave and **Yemi** *stops him.*

Yemi   NAH NAH NAH, you can't.

Ikudayisi   Now you want me to stay eh, ehh? Why?

Yemi   I'm sorry innit, I didn't mean it.

Ikudayisi   You meant it. Oh, you are evil! I'm going back home. Let the police come and catch you here.

Yemi   I'm not going to beg you, you nah.

Ikudayisi   I don't care. You are crazy.

Yemi *stands in his way.*

Yemi   Use your head. If you go home without the milk, *we* will get in trouble.

Ikudayisi   NO! *You* will get in trouble. I will just tell her you are misbehaving.

Yemi   And *I* will tell her you tried to steal somink.

Ikudayisi   That's a lie! You are the one causing trouble outside here. I was not part of it, I never did anything.

Yemi   SO! But how will she know dat?

Ikudayisi   Cos it a lie.

Yemi   Who has she known longer? Trust me, blud, don't test me.

Blackout.

Scene Three

Ikudayisi *and* **Yemi** *have now walked to a different part of the estate.*

Ikudayisi   We have been walking for long-oh.

Yemi   Stop your complaining.

Ikudayisi   So, how far are we going to go before we go back home?

Yemi   She said not to come back without the milk. What about *dat*, don't you understand?

Ikudayisi   But all the shops are closed.

Yemi   You always point out the obvious, innit. Indian shops are always open on a bank holiday in this country. They are money-orientated people, they will do anything for money.

Ikudayisi   What, like the other shopkeeper did? Have you forgotten he didn't care if you had money, he didn't want you in his shop.

Yemi   No! It was *me* who didn't want to go into *his* shop.

Ikudayisi   Your memory is short.

Yemi   Whatever.

Ikudayisi   So where is this other shop? I'm tired! We have been walking, walking, and I cannot see de shop. I don't want to walk no more, I want to go back home.

He sits down.

Yemi   I don't know what you are complaining bout. Don't you have to walk miles in Nigeria to get water? And now you're in England you going on like you can't even walk. We haven't even gone far. That's the problem with you people straight from the bush, you get to this country and want bare luxuries. What, you think, a horse and carriage is gonna come and carry you around? I was raised in these ends so I know where I'm going.

He starts walking but **Ikudayisi** *remains seated.*

Yemi   GET UP! You know how Mum stays, so why do you act all dumb? If we go back empty-handed, what do you think she will do?

Ikudayisi   I don't care. You are de one dat is scared of punishment.

Yemi   I'm not scared.

Ikudayisi   So let's go back home then ah ah now.

Yemi   No. We've been stuck inside da house for a week and now we are out, you want to go back in. Are you mad? You GO! I'm not going till I get this stuff, and if that means going to bare different shops, I'm going.

Ikudayisi (*looking around*)   It's only now you are saying I should go. Do I know where to go? We have been walking, walking, walking . . .

Yemi   Boy! If you don't know the way – I guess you got to stay den, innit!

Ikudayisi   *Ah ah koda now.* [That is not good.]

Yemi   WHAT DID YOU SAY?

Ikudayisi *starts laughing.*

Yemi   I SAID, WHAT DID YOU SAY?

Ikudayisi   You are Nigerian, you should know.

Yemi   What are you talking about? You know I don't understand.

Ikudayisi   It's not my problem.

Yemi   I hate it when you speak dat language.

Ikudayisi   Why, are you ashamed of being Nigerian? You can't change what you are.

Yemi   I'm not. I SAID I'M NOT!

Offstage there is giggling, then two girls come onstage. **Yemi** *notices them and runs up to them.*

Yemi   What's up, Armani, Paris?

Paris   Hi, Yemi.

Yemi   You're look Chung today, Paris.

Paris   Thanks!

Yemi   So where you lovely ladies going?

Paris   Nowhere, we were just about –

Armani   None of your business.

Pause.

Yemi   So, Paris, when are we gonna link up?

Armani   She's not! (*To* **Paris**.) Come, man, let's go.

Paris   I can talk for myself, you nah.

Armani   Why would you . . . ?

Ikudayisi *has bopped up to* **Yemi** *and is profiling behind his shoulder. He looks at the girls in admiration.*

Ikudayisi (*in a dodgy American accent*)   Yo, Yemi, you're not gonna introduce me to your friends?

Armani   Whoo's dis?

Yemi *shrugs* **Ikudayisi** *off.*

Yemi   I don't know him.

Ikudayisi   Ah ah . . . Oluyemi Adewale, so you are going to pretend we are not bruddas?

Paris   You got a brother? I never knew dat.

Yemi   No, he's my brother, but not my –

Armani   I never knew you was African.

Paris   You don't look African.

Ikudayisi   I don't look African?

The girls laugh.

Armani   No, *you* look African. Yemi don't look African.

Ikudayisi   *Ori e o pe.* [Your head is not correct.]

Armani   Wat did he say?

Yemi   I don't know, I don't speak dat language. What does an African look like? What is it you're tryna say?

Armani   You come from his country – what did he say?

Yemi   What does an *African* look like?

Armani   That's not what he said.

Yemi   No, *I* said what does an African look like.

Armani   I don't care!

Yemi   Well, I do. What does one look like?

Armani   An African, innit. Now what did he say?

Paris *nudges* **Armani**.

Paris   Lauw it, Armani.

Yemi   Nah, tell her to say what she mean.

Paris   She doesn't mean nothing.

Yemi   Let Armani speak.

Paris   It's just –

Armani   *Forget* it, man, I was only saying you don't look African, innit. What your problem? It's a compliment.

Yemi   *Compliment?*

Armani   You should be happy you don't look like dem. Be grateful you don't have big lips and big nose.

Yemi   What?

Paris   Armani!

Armani   It the truth, why am I going to sugar-coat it for? You're lucky you're not black black.

Ikudayisi   All of us are black. We are all from Africa-oh.

Armani   Nah, later, I'm from *yard*, bruv.

Ikudayisi (*laughing*)   D' backyard? (*To* **Yemi**.) *Werre.* [Crazy.]

He continues laughing.

Armani   What did he say now?

Yemi   What is wrong with having big lips?

He begins to feel his lips.

Armani   Why you covering up for him for? Dat's not what he said.

Yemi   I told you before, I don't speak dat language.

Ikudayisi   *Omo iranu koti e mo kun ko.* [Stupid girl, don't even know nothing.]

He laughs again.

Armani   But *you're* African –

Yemi I was *born* here!

Paris He is laughing hard dough. Seriously, Yemi, what did he say?

Yemi I don't know.

Ikudayisi (*to* **Yemi**) Backyard. *Omo jaku jaku.* [This silly girl.]

Armani Yemi, are you tryna take da piss?

She moves towards **Yemi**.

Yemi Back up, man. I ain't the one saying or doing anything, he's the one speaking. Speak to him.

Armani *moves still closer to* **Yemi**.

Yemi You're starting to get on my nerves now. Just duss –

Armani Are you taking the piss?

Ikudayisi *Omo girl e omo jaku jaku.* [This silly girl.] *Oti so ro so ro ju.* [She talks too much.] *Werre.* [Crazy.]

Armani Listen, Adebabatunde, or watever your name is, yeah, we are in England so tell ya people to speak fucking English if they got something to say.

Yemi IS THE WORDS EVEN COMING OUT OF MY MOUTH? I TOLD YOU I DON'T SPEAK THAT LANGUAGE. GET OUT MY FACE.

Armani AND WHAT YOU GONNA DO, YOU AFRICAN BUBU?

Yemi (*starts squaring up into her face*) Who da fuck you talking to like that?

Armani I'm talking to *you*!

Yemi You better watch your mouth, yeah.

Armani What what what, what are you gonna do?

Yemi Just watch your mouth.

Paris   Yous lot, man . . .

Ikudayisi   Please, let's not fight –

Armani   Nah, later, man, chatting like he gonna do something. Make him come and do something. (*To* **Yemi**.) If you're gonna do something, do something, innit.

Yemi   Move. I ain't got time for you.

He turns to leave.

Armani   See, you're just a pussy, all you African people dem are. Jus go home and eat your jelly and rice.

Yemi   WHAT?

Armani   What, you got problem understanding English now? (*She puts on an African accent.*) EH EH, do I need to speak in your language –

Yemi *goes for* **Armani** *and pokes her in the head.* **Paris** *tries to stop him and gets pushed to the ground.*

Paris   No, don't . . .

Armani   AHH . . .

Ikudayisi   No no no, Yemi, you cannot hit a lady. (*To* **Paris**.) Yo, mammy, you OK?

Paris   Yeah, I'm cool.

Armani   Oh my God, oh my God, you just touch me, you just touch me! Nah nah, I ain't having dat.

She tries to go for **Yemi** *but* **Ikudayisi** *holds her back.*

Ikudayisi (*to* **Armani**)   Yo princess, you gotta calm down.

Armani   Don't touch me, don't touch me! Move, man, don't come near me.

Ikudayisi   Let's go, Yemi.

Yemi   Shut up, man. (*To* **Armani**.) You started this. I ain't going nowhere.

Armani Just watch, yeah, fink sey you can touch mi and get away with it. Watch wen my man hears bout this, you think you're gonna be alive? My man gonna have you up, he is gonna slash you up. You think you're a bad now, yeah, yeah, yeah. Watch, yeah, watch.

Yemi I'm watching.

Paris Please, you two –

Armani Is it, is it. Mans don't lay their hands on me and live to see the next day, you know. People like you get taken and buried where no one can't find you. Even your mum's gonna be searching for your body, she not even gonna know where to look, yeah, yeah.

Yemi Ohhh, *gangsta* now, is it?

Armani I ain't tryna be gangsta, I'm just telling you how it is. You made the worst mistake of your life today, the worst mistake. This is the beginning, blud, this is the beginning. Living on this estate is gonna be the hell from today. Everywhere you go you're gonna have to watch your back. You see, you see, you forget, yeah, I know bare people on these ends. Once everyone knows what you tried to do today, what, you're done for. You better pack your bags and go back to Africa now.

Yemi SHUT YOUR MOUTH. SHUT UP AND DUSS. GO GET YOUR MAN. THINK MANS LIKE ME IS SHOOK?

Paris Yemi, please –

Armani Nah, don't beg babatunde for nothing, let him talk, cos everything he is saying now my man's gonna hear bout it. (*To* **Yemi**.) Just watch you, bubu.

Yemi *goes for* **Armani** *again.*

Blackout.

Scene Four

Yemi *and* **Ikudayisi** *have moved to another part of the estate.* **Yemi** *is sitting down with his legs up on a bench and his bum on the top half. He is still very angry about his run-in with* **Armani**. **Ikudayisi** *watches him and when he registers that* **Yemi** *is not moving he too sits down on the bench.*

Ikudayisi   Yemi, next time you should not hit a woman-oh.

Yemi   She's not a woman, she's a yout.

Ikudayisi   You should try and talk it out.

Yemi   You saw her – I didn't even get a word in. She is always running up her mouth. And for the record, I never hit her, I only *revered* her. And if it wasn't for you this wouldn't have happened in the first place.

Ikudayisi   I didn't do anything.

Yemi   You were talking in that language that nobody *understands*! I told you already I didn't like it – see what you started.

Ikudayisi   She was talking nonsense.

Yemi   She is *such* an idiot.

Pause.

And so is her man too, bout she saying she gonna get him on to me. Make him come, I'm ready for him, blud. I'm not afraid of no one.

Ikudayisi   Just calm down. Don't go looking for trouble.

Yemi   I ain't looking for no trouble. All I'm saying is, if it comes I'm ready! Come, man, get up – we ain't got time to sit down.

Ikudayisi   But . . . you . . . please let's just stay here for a minute, all that punishment I have been doing today has hurt my legs. I am tired-oh.

Yemi   So? So am I.

Ikudayisi   So let's rest. What is the big hurry?

Yemi   Look at the time. It getting late.

Ikudayisi   I don't have a watch.

Yemi   Like that should stop you – can't you just look at the sun and know the time?

Ikudayisi   Ah ah, Yemi, what *nonsense* are you talking? You are so ignorant! *Ki lo she e?* [What is wrong with you?]

Yemi   Why do you always mix English with Nigerian?

Ikudayisi   It's not called Nigerian – the language is Yoruba.

Yemi   I don't care what it is.

Ikudayisi   *Kini problem e?* [What is your problem?]

Yemi   You don't listen. See, that what I mean. Don't you know when you speak nobody round here understand a word you're saying.

Ikudayisi   You can learn if you want.

Yemi   Dat's long.

Pause.

Ikudayisi   What was that jelly and rice she was talking about?

Yemi   Who?

Ikudayisi   Dat girl.

Yemi   Oh, dat idiot. She was tryna say *jollof rice*, innit.

Ikudayisi   How can jollof rice be jelly?

Yemi   Exactly!

Ikudayisi   *Omo jaku jaku.* [Silly girl.]

Yemi (*laughs*)   That word is funny. Dat's what you called her innit? Did you see her face when you said that?

Ikudayisi   Of course now, she looked like this.

He mimics **Armani**'s *face and they both laugh.*

Yemi   What was the other word you used?

Ikudayisi   Which one? I used a lot.

Yemi   That word beginning with 'w'.

Ikudayisi   Oh, *werre*.

Yemi   Yeah, dat one is funny too. I heard Mum saying that on the phone a few times. What does it mean?

Ikudayisi   It means crazy.

Yemi   For real. *H*ow do you say it?

Ikudayisi   *Werre*.

Yemi   *Warrri*.

Ikudayisi   No, *way* as in 'way' and *ray* as in 'ray'.

Yemi   *Way-ray*.

Ikudayisi   Yes, that's close.

Yemi   I guess that word is alright. Teach me ano – Nah, forget it, man.

Ikudayisi   Stop fighting it – you want to learn Yoruba.

Yemi   I don't.

Ikudayisi   It's easy.

Yemi   No man, I don't want to know.

Ikudayisi   Why?

Yemi   What is the point? When in Rome do as the Roman.

Ikudayisi   What do you mean?

Yemi   Meaning, what is the point of learning to speak *your* language when I don't even live in *that* country. We are in England. I only need to know how to speak English.

Ikudayisi   It's a nice language.

Yemi   No, it's not, it's not like it's Spanish or anything – now *dat's* a sexy language, I'll learn dat *any day*.

Ikudayisi   Yoruba is sexy too. Back home when I use it on the girl Kai! They come running, and I have to beat them away with a stick.

*He moves towards **Yemi** and demonstrates.*

Ikudayisi   Come here and let me show you. *Omo ge ki lo ruko e?* [Sexy girl, what's your name?]

Yemi   Move, you batty man.

Ikudayisi   Stop your shakara. Don't try and fight it. Yoruba can hypnotise you. When it does, there is nothing you can do. Come here, stop trying to resist it. *Omo ge, omo ge.* [Sexy girls, sexy girls.]

Yemi   Move, I'm not convinced. There is nothing sexy bout the language.

Ikudayisi   It bad-oh.

Yemi   What's bad?

Ikudayisi   That you are not embracing your culture. What does Mum say when you talk like this?

Yemi   She don't say nothing. She don't care bout speaking African either.

Ikudayisi   Ah ah, that not true, she speaks *Yoruba* all the time.

Yemi   No, she only started when you came. Before, she was forever speaking English. I never knew she could even speak in that language. Don't you hear, when she is on the phone she acts more English than me?

Ikudayisi   Come here, let me teach you Yoruba. Try it – *omo ge, omo ge.*

Yemi   Get lost!

Ikudayisi   You can use it on dat girl's friend. I saw da way you were looking at her, your mouth touch the floor.

Yemi   Shut up! Move, man.

Ikudayisi   I know you have never kissed a girl –

Yemi   What?

*An **Old Lady** enters with some shopping bags. She is halfway across when she notices **Yemi** and **Ikudayisi**. She stops in her tracks and contemplates turning back, but is too afraid to move.*

Ikudayisi   Before, you can use Yoruba on her, she will lie down at your feet, treat you like a king!

Yemi   See, that's why I can't stand you, you're going on like you know everything bout me – you don't know shit.

Ikudayisi   I'm only playing. I know you have kissed plenty of girls.

Yemi   Shut up, man! You don't know nothing about me . . . You going like –

Ikudayisi *notices the **Old Lady** now and jumps off the bench.*

Ikudayisi   Ma, sorry, don't you want to sit down?

Yemi   Ahhhhhh –

He rolls his eyes, takes out his phone and starts playing with it.

Old Lady   No no no no. I'm OK!

Ikudayisi   I can see you are tired – please come and sit down.

*The **Old Lady** stays still, scared.*

Ikudayisi (*to **Yemi***)   Move now.

Yemi   What? NO! What for?

Ikudayisi   For this lady – she needs to sit down.

Yemi   What is wrong wid you?

Old Lady   I'm not looking for trouble. (*To* **Ikudayisi**) OK, I just wanna go home.

Yemi   Exactly. Let her go.

Ikudayisi   No, it's not OK. (*To* **Yemi**.) You're going to have to move your feet.

Yemi   She don't need a seat.

Ikudayisi   Yemi, where is your manners?

He snatches **Yemi***'s phone and the* **Old Lady**, *frightened, drops her shopping.* **Ikudayisi** *goes to help.*

Yemi   Give it back.

Old Lady   Please don't touch me – I told you, I'm not looking for trouble.

Yemi   Give me the phone back – the battery low.

Ikudayisi   Ma, let me help you.

The **Old Lady** *starts edging backwards, raising her voice.*

Old Lady   Stay away! Stay away.

Yemi (*to* **Ikudayisi**)   What wrong with you?

Old Lady   Please . . .

Ikudayisi   I'm only helping.

Old Lady   Please, I just wanna go home.

Yemi   Go.

Ikudayisi   We can't let her go – her bags have broken.

He tries to help her gather up the things that have fallen on the ground.

Old Lady   OH GOD!

Yemi   Are you blind? She don't want you to come near her.

Old Lady   I know what you're trying to do, you can take it.

Yemi   What you talking about?

Old Lady Anything, have anything.

Yemi Oh my Dayz, see what I'm saying?

Old Lady Please, please, I just wanna go home.

Yemi DAYISI, JUST MOVE AWAY FROM HER!

Old Lady Have it, have it, anything you want.

Ikudayisi *moves away from the bag.*

Yemi Stop making noise, man, no one is near you.

Ikudayisi Ma, I'm sorry, I only trying to help.

Old Lady Stay away from me! STAY AWAY!

She picks up her bag but is too frightened to move.

Yemi Go, blud!

*The **Old Lady** scurries off the stage.*

Yemi (*to* **Ikudayisi**) You're so dumb.

Ikudayisi What are you talking about? You shouldn't talk
so harsh to her – she is not your mate.

Yemi What?

Blackout.

Scene Five

It is late afternoon, around five o'clock. **Razer**, **Flamer**, **Armani**
and **Paris** *are hanging around on another part of the estate, drinking and
making noise.*

Armani . . . and then he tried to get rude, can you believe
it? He put his hand on me, you nah.

Paris To be fair, he only revered you in the head.

Armani So what, he's your man now.

Paris NO!

Armani   You meant to have my back.

Paris   I'm just saying what happened.

Armani   You calling me a liar?

Paris   No . . .

Armani   So what you saying?

Paris   Nothing, forget it.

Armani   Nah man, I'm not forgetting it. You been like this all day. Say what you got to say, Paris, say what you got to say.

Paris   Nothing.

Armani   It better be.

Paris   What better be?

Armani   I'm just saying, innit. You're meant be my friend. And friends always have each other's backs, no matter what. Know whose side you're on.

Razer   Stop talking to her like dat – Paris is your girl, man.

Flamer   She's always got your back.

Armani   Not today she didn't. Anyway, back to the story . . .

A big boy with a hood start is slowly walking towards them.

Paris   I wonder who that is.

Armani   ERHH UM! Hello!

Flamer *and* **Razer** *ignore* **Armani***, turn round and draw out their knives.*

Paris   What is wrong with you? What's that for? Put them away.

Flamer   Mans can't be too careful on the ends. We can't let our guards down just cos we are home.

The figure is still walking towards them suspiciously.

Mans better identify themselves before they reach any closer, you know.

Blazer   What's up, my youth?

Everyone recognises the voice immediately and lets their guard down, except **Armani** *who kisses her teeth.*

Razer *and* **Flamer** *burst into the song and start dancing. They put their knivees away.*

Razer *and* **Flamer**   Who you calling my yout, my yout?

Armani   I'm not anyone yout but my mother's.

Blazer   Shut up.

Armani *kisses her teeth and rolls her eyes.* (*To* **Razer** *and* **Flamer**.) You should have seen you mans' faces, you were shook.

Flamer   Nah man, we were prepared.

Flamer *shows* **Blazer** *his knife.*

Blazer   Nice, nice, it's good to see you mans are following rule number one.

Razer   Yep! You always got to watch your back –

Flamer   – cos your enemies are always closer than you think.

Blazer   Ahhh, my youts are learning fast.

He nudges **Flamer** *and* **Razer**.

Armani   Oh please, you ain't teaching anyone anything worthwhile.

Blazer   Every time I see you, you always got something to say. I am the preacher on these ends, so you better listen.

Paris   Preacher! You're funny.

Armani   He is not funny, Paris!

Blazer   Whatever. (*To* **Flamer** *and* **Razer**.) So what's popping, my soldiers?

Flamer   Nothing – Armani was just telling us bout her run-in wid Yemi.

Blazer   Which Yemi?

Paris   The one who lives on Farnborough Way –

Armani   Oh yeah, before we got rudely interrupted. As I was saying, *dat babatunde*, yeah –

Blazer (*to* **Flamer**)   I thought you said Yemi?

Flamer   Yeah –

Armani   Excuse me, I'm talking now –

Blazer   Hold on. Armani, are you trying to take da piss?

Armani   As I was saying –

Blazer   What, *all* African are called *babatunde*, yeah?

Razer   Blud, she ain't saying dat.

Blazer   So, what she tryna say? Cos I swear Flamer said she was talking bout Yemi and now she calling him *babatunde*!

Flamer   It's just a figure of speech.

Blazer   Nah, it's rude. (*To* **Armani**.) When you're in my presence you got to speak properly. If you talking bout Yemi, call him Yemi. If not –

Armani   Oh my God, yeah, why are you longing everything out? I just want to finish my story.

Blazer   Nah!

Armani   But I'm talking.

Blazer   No, I'm talking now. Listen and understand. If you talking bout a specific person say their name.

Armani   Cha, man, I'll do whatever I wanna do.

Blazer *moves towards* **Armani** *and stands really close to her face.*

Blazer   No, you do as I say. You're talking bout Yemi, his name is Yemi.

Unafraid of his presence, **Armani** *moves away and continues talking.*

Armani   His name can be called Kunta Kinte for all I care.
I don't give a shit.

Blazer   You need a lesson in history then, cos Kunta Kinte
is from Gambia.

Armani   I don't care, I don't care. I wasn't even talking to
you in the first place. I know all history I need to know, you
ain't got to teach me anything new. All I need to know is, I'm
from yard!

Blazer   I've seen your mum – she's *white*!

Armani   So my dad is black.

Blazer   And?

Armani   And he is Jamaican. So dat makes me Jamaican.

Blazer   Have you *even* seen him? Probably don't even know
what he looks like.

Razer   Lauw it, blud, you don't have to bring her dad into
this.

Blazer (*to* **Armani**)   I've never even seen you set foot outside
this estate, let alone go to another country, so how can you say
you're Jamaican? Do you have a passport? Do you even know
what a passport looks like?

Flamer   Blazer, man, it's not called for.

Blazer   Nah, blud, she's too rude and needs to learn her
place. If her mum doesn't know how to teach her bout respect,
I'll teach her. (*To* **Armani**.) When someone older is talking to
you, you keep your mouth shut. Speak only when spoken to.
Know your place. Respect your elders.

Armani   You're not even related to me.

Blazer   SHUT UP! I said speak *only* when you're spoken to.

Armani   What are you talking about? You *are* speaking to
me.

Blazer (*to* **Razer**)   Tell your girl to mind out, you know.

Armani   I should mind out, I should mind out. (*To* **Razer**.) You not gonna say nothing? Look how I've been quiet when this boy been shouting at me. When are you going to step in?

Razer   He's only playing. (*To* **Blazer**.) Ain't you, Blazer?

Blazer   Blud, I'm not! Your girl needs to mind out.

They sit in awkward silence.

Paris (*to* **Blazer**)   I thought Kunta Kinte was a made-up name.

Blazer   Nah, he was real.

Paris   How do you know that?

Blazer   Cos I read. (*Staring at* **Armani**.) Unlike some people. And does anyone have a problem with dat?

Razer   Lauw it, blud, man, this is not a history class.

Flamer   Yeah, let's just keep the peace.

Blazer   So what, *you two* got a problem with me?

Razer   Course not, blud, you know I'm easy. I don't want no trouble, innit. We're one big fam out ere.

Flamer   Yeah, man, just take it easy.

Armani   He ain't my family.

Razer   Armani!

Armani   Look, yeah, I don't know why you lot are begging it with him for. (*To* **Blazer**.) You wasn't even invited to this conversation, *Blazer*!

Blazer *stares at* **Armani** *and* **Razer** *jumps in.*

Razer   Armani, man, please.

Armani   Why can't I talk? No, I'll speak when I want to.

Razer   Just lauw it, man. Sometimes you really need to know when to keep your mouth shut.

Armani   What, like you?

Razer   We were having a good time before.

Armani   And am I the one who was spoiling it?

Razer   Ahhhh, man.

Armani   I don't know what you making noise for. I swear you people forgot this is a free country. And in a free country people can talk freely. We are not in no third world. I can do what I want. I ain't afraid of no one.

Razer   ARMANI!

Flamer *and* **Paris** *start laughing at* **Armani** *and* **Razer** *arguing.* **Blazer** *gets up to leave.*

Flamer   You gone already?

Blazer   Yeah, man, this is too childish for me. And before I do something I might regret –

He looks long and hard at **Armani**.

– it's best I'm off. When you mans are done here meet me up at frontline. There is something I need you two to work on.

Flamer   Yeah, fam.

Blazer   One.

He nudges the boys.

See you later.

Paris   Yeah, see you later.

Blazer *exits.*

Armani *looks at* **Paris** *and gives her a dirty look.*

Armani   I hate him, you nah.

Razer   He can ruin the mood sometimes.

Flamer   So can your girl, you know.

Flamer, **Razer** *and* **Paris** *start laughing.*

Paris   I like Blazer, I think he is cool.

Armani   Yeah, you would.

Flamer   Nah, she right, most times he is alright. But he likes to talk a lot. We all know it shit, but it don't matter. When he talks just let him talk, innit.

Armani   Why? He not my dad. I'm not gonna shut *my* mouth cos he's around. He don't control me. No one does.

Flamer   But you ain't got to stir things up.

Armani   Stop sitting on the fence and defending him. You don't have to worry, your *boss* is gone, he can't hear me. You can now tell the truth bout what you really feel, speak your mind. You won't get arrest for it, you know. This is a *free* country.

Flamer   That's your problem, Armani, you don't listen. Didn't you hear me? I'm agreeing with you, and he ain't my boss.

Armani   You could have fooled me. When he comes around you lot start shaking.

Razer   Not me.

He nudges **Flamer**.

Armani   Whatever! He rules you too. Cos you chat different bout him when it just me and you. Den when he is in your face you're nuff quiet like a likkle biatch! I'm surprise you ain't following him around on a leash.

Razer   It's not like dat man – shut up.

Paris   I think he chats nuff sense. He is cool with me. He got a nice way about him, I love the way he proud bout where he from.

Armani   What, like being so fucking proud to be African but then calling himself Blazer? I bet you don't even know what his real name is.

Razer *laughs.*

Razer   She's right you nah. I can't remember his real name. Do you, Flamer?

Flamer   Yeah, course I know.

Armani   What is it?

Flamer   It's one long ass-funky name like Oluade . . .
Oluwaye . . . ahhh, I can't remember it.

Paris   Why does dat matter doe? He may not like people
knowing his real name. Most people never know how to
pronounce African names properly anyway. It probably
frustrates him. Anyways, Blazer is only his street name. (*To*
Razer *and* **Flamer**.) Not dat many people know yous lot
names either, do dey?

Armani   You're so stupid – that's not the reason.

Paris   What the reason, then?

Armani   *He is ashamed!*

Paris   He's not, he always talking bout Africa. How can he
be ashamed?

Armani   *So* why doesn't *he* hang around his people den?
Everyone *I* see him with is West Indian.

Paris   Dat don't mean nothing.

Armani   Look, Paris, yeah, you're always sticking up for dem
people. I told you once already today – know your sides! You
forget back in da days they sold us off as slaves, you nah.

Flamer   I ain't no slave. My nan told me she was invited to
this country, you get me?

Razer   Yeah, same here, fam.

Flamer *and* **Razer**   WINDRUSH!

They nudge each other.

Armani   You two are so dumb. We are all slaves, all of us
from the West Indies. Dat why I don't like African, cos they
sold us off to da white man, and den stayed in Africa living
as kings and queens, while all my ancestors had to work hard.

Razer, **Flamer** *and* **Paris**   WHAT?!

Armani   Nah, blud, I'm not happy with dat and I'm not having it either. You can go around loving off your African people but I stick with my own.

Paris   You have it so messed up. Everything you're saying don't make no sense. It doesn't even go like dat and furthermore you're half white . . . so . . . .. do you hate white people as well?

Armani   No, eh, my mum's white, *hello*!

Paris   You're not making any sense, Armani. You can't just be one-sided. How can you hate African people but not the white people who were also involved in slavery?

Armani   Cos slavery started in Africa.

Paris   But white people *went* to Africa and took them from their land.

Armani   So, what, *you* love African but hate white people now?

Paris   I didn't say dat.

Armani   Well *that's* what I'm hearing.

Paris   No, that's what you want to hear. You're not getting my point.

Armani   Yeah I am, yeah I am, it's all coming out now.

Paris   You're still not understanding me –

Armani   I'm getting exactly what you're tryna say.

Paris   You're not.

Armani   Yes, I am. It's all coming to light now. Now I understand the way that you been acting towards me. I'm so stupid, I should have seen it before.

Paris   What are you talking bout?

Armani   You're a *racist*, Paris.

Paris   What?

Razer   No she's not, man.

Flamer   She is far from racist – Paris is the nicest person we know.

Armani   Yes she is, YES SHE IS – she said it with her own mouth.

Paris   Said what? I never said anything.

Armani   Oh my God, you're a liar too.

Paris (*to* **Razer** *and* **Flamer**)   You two woz here. Did I say I hate white people?

Flamer *and* **Razer**   No.

Armani   I don't care, you can't backtrack now, I know you're a racist.

Paris   But if I'm racist you're racist too, then.

Armani   No, far from it.

Paris   Yes, you are. Hating African is *just as* racist as hating white people. So if you're calling me a racist, you're racist too.

Armani   That's not even the same.

Paris   Why – is it one rule for you and another for me? You can't have it your way *all the time*, Armani.

Armani   At least I know why you don't like me now.

Razer   How can she not like you? You been friends for years.

Armani   That's just a cover-up.

Paris   You really don't know what you are talking bout.

Armani   Yeah, I do. Things like this happen all the time. That's why I hate being friends with girls.

Paris   But I've never had a problem with you before *or* now.

Armani   I know where this hatred comes from anyway. It's jealousy.

Paris   What are you talking bout *now*?

Armani   Dark-skinned girls always have problems with light-skinned girls.

Flamer   Ahhh, come on.

Armani   It's the truth. All dark-skinned girls are like dat, they are forever hating –

Flamer   Paris is not like dat – why would she hate, she pretty herself –

Armani   They forget us light-skinned girl are not to blame, you nah. We don't get to pick our parents.

Paris   First I'm a racist and now I am hater. Make up your mind, Armani.

Armani   Ask Razer – he knows what I'm talking bout.

Razer   What?

Paris   What's she talking bout, Razer?

Razer   Don't get me involved in dis.

Paris   What, Razer, you think I hate light-skinned girls?

Razer   I've never said dat.

Armani   Don't lie now.

Razer   I'm not, don't get me involved in yout madness.

Paris   Well, everything you say is wrong. I haven't got any problems and never had one either.

Armani   You're such a liar. At least everyone here gets to know it now.

Paris   Stop talking rubbish, Armani.

Armani   I'm not, it's the truth!

Paris   It's not me that tryna be something dat I'm not.

Armani   What you saying?

Paris   Exactly what I just said!

Flamer   Take it easy, girls.

Paris   Nah! I'm fed up of being quiet. If you want me to get everything out in the open, *I'll* be real with you.

Flamer   Paris, lauw it, it's not worth it.

Razer   Girls, man, you're meant to be friends.

Paris   No, I'm fed up of this. It's my time to speak now.

Armani   Speak then – ain't no one holding you back.

Paris   I think it's *you* with the big problem.

Razer   Keep the peace, man, keep the peace.

Paris   But it not your fault cos *all* mixed-raced girls are confused.

Flamer   Paris!

Paris   I said girls.

Armani   Nah, later. Not me.

Paris   Especially you! You don't know what to identify yourself with. Should you be on the white side, should you be on the black side – *you don't know.* You try and act like you're blacker dan anybody else, but then you contradict yourself cos you go on like it's a bad thing for me to look black, or anyone else at that. I've always been cool with myself and even cooler wid you. When other *light-skinned* girls have chatted shit bout you, I've been the one to defend your ass. But I'm the hater – cos I'm dark-skinned! You just don't get it. You are *so* confused!

Flamer   Ooohhh, see what you started, Armani. I bet you thought Paris never had no mouth.

Armani   Oh my God, you're so funny – is that what you think?

Paris   No, it what I know. You forget sometimes how long I've known you and what you *used* to be like. How would you know about the black-hair shops if I didn't take you there? Cos your *mum* never knew what to do with your hair. You were walking around with a picky Afro *until the day I met you*! I've still got pictures in my house! I'm the one who still braids your hair! And who taught you about the dance moves that they did in Jamaica, cos Blazer's right – you ain't never been there, or anywhere else apart from *here*. And furthermore, I been to your yard and the *only* food your mum showed you how to cook was beans on toast! Remember – I introduced you to rice and peas. So don't get it twisted!

Flamer   You got told!

Armani   WHAT? SHUT UP! She is such a liar. She never taught me nothink. Come say that to my face. COME SAY THAT TO MY FACE.

Armani *tries to go for* **Paris** *but* **Razer** *and* **Flamer** *hold her back.* **Paris** *stands her ground.*

Paris   If it's a lie why you acting all mad for? It shouldn't be bothering you. You should just be cool. You're the big bad Armani. You're always right – right?

Armani   How can you try and say you taught me bout hair? Look at my hair and look at yours. (*To* **Razer**.) Look, Razer, look.

Paris   *So*, as I said, it's my influence.

Razer *and* **Flamer** *start laughing.*

Armani   What, come say that to my face.

Paris   I am. The truth hurts, doesn't it?

Blackout.

Scene Six

Yemi *is on another side of the estate,* **Ikudayisi** *is offstage, trying to catch up with him and calling his name.* **Yemi** *does not respond and goes and sits down on a wall, playing with his phone.*

Ikudayisi (*off*)   Yemi, Yemi, Yemi!

He comes onstage and is shocked to see **Yemi** *sitting down. He walks over to him.*

Ikudayisi   So is this where you have been all this time?

Yemi *ignores him.*

Ikudayisi   So, did you not hear me calling your name?

Yemi *still ignores him.*

Ikudayisi   Yemi! Can you not hear me asking you questions?

Yemi   JUST LEAVE ME ALONE.

Ikudayisi   No – what is your problem?

Yemi   AHHH, MAN!

Ikudayisi   Are you having some kind of breakdown?

Yemi   JUST LEAVE ME ALONE, leave me alone.

Ikudayisi   No, we need to talk about what happened before. You shouldn't have talked to that old lady like dat.

Yemi   What, are you dizzy?

Ikudayisi   She is as old as our grandmother and you were rude.

Yemi   She was *scared* of you! Why can't you just go away?

Ikudayisi   No, I'm your brother, I'm here to stay.

Yemi   Why did you have to come? Why couldn't you just stay in Nigeria. Ever since you come . . . I liked it how it was!

Ikudayisi   Why are you being like this?

Yemi   Why can't you just go away?

Ikudayisi   No, I'm here to stay. I couldn't wait to come, just to see you. To see my younger brother and this is de way you are treating me. If this was Nigeria –

Yemi   This is not Nigeria. Why do you think you could just come over here and take over?

Ikudayisi   I'M NOT TRYING TO TAKE OVER. I just want to be a part of your life.

Yemi   You come here and act the way you do, and think . . . and think . . . everyone should just accept that. All these stupid things you keep on doing like speaking in that language and trying to be friendly to everyone does not work here. People don't want you to be nice to them. YOU NEED TO UNDERSTAND THIS IS NOT NIGERIA, things are different here.

Ikudayisi   What do you mean?

Yemi   You can't do what you do there, *here*.

Ikudayisi   I can't be friendly?

Yemi   NO, you can't! This country is not like dat. People will look at you like you are crazy. You just need to mind your own business. Don't watch no one else.

Ikudayisi   That's nonsense. You are lost.

Yemi   NO, you're lost. You think being the way you are is cool. It's not! You're a joke. People in this country laugh at people like you – they find your look and your accent funny. They think you're a joke. But you can't *even* see dat.

Ikudayisi   That's nonsense. Since I have been here people have been nice to me – it's you that has been having problems.

Yemi   Are you stupid? You almost gave an old lady a heart attack. She thought you were robbing her.

Ikudayisi   What?

Yemi   If you stopped living in la-la land for once, you would see that. Stop being stupid and look around you.

Ikudayisi   You this silly boy. See what? What is there to see? You are not thinking straight. Your mind-set needs to change.

Yemi   You're the one who needs to change, not me! Stop all the 'we are the world' shit you keep on doing, and understand that in order to get along on this estate, in this country, you need to stop being you, Dayisi!

Ikudayisi   I can't change – being a Nigerian is what I am.

Yemi   I can't help you then, cos you're never gonna fit in.

Ikudayisi   That's a lie. I fit it well, I get on with everyone.

Yemi   Look! Take some good advice: you're not going to get far how you are right now – trust me, I know this.

Ikudayisi   You are strange-oh, you talk too much rubbish.

Yemi   No, I'm chatting sense and it best you listen to me, cos –

Ikudayisi   No, you listen to me. You are trying to educate someone who is already educated. I know who I am and what I stand for. I will not change for anyone. Ahhh, you disappoint me-oh, I didn't know your problem run so deep.

Yemi   You're buzzing. I ain't got time for this.

He turns to walk away.

Ikudayisi   Dat's your problem – you don't want to face up to nothing. You talk so much nonsense, but the minute someone else has something to say, you want to go.

Yemi   Shut up, man. What would you know? You don't even know me, man. What! WHAT! You been here two months and you think you can tell me bout me. I don't expect you to understand coming from a backward country.

Ikudayisi   Take that back! Nigeria is not backward.

Yemi   Uhhh, yes it is. Don't get it twisted, blud, just cos I ain't been there don't mean I ain't heard the stories. Duh! Mum's always talking bout you lot not always having electricity. How can you tell me dat not backward?

Ikudayisi   You don't understand . . . It's only when Nepa [*Nigerian Electricity Board*] takes the light. We have generators.

Yemi   But the lights are not on 24/7, are they? I bet you ain't even got traffic lights – how can you, with no electricity? Is there even cars in Africa? Do you even have houses?

Ikudayisi   You dis one who has never set foot in Nigeria and is now talking like you discovered it. You are de one that is backward and confused, talking bad about your mother homeland like that. Be careful God does not strike you now.

Yemi   Shut up. I don't even know why you getting offended for. You don't live there any more, you couldn't wait to come here. So everything you're saying is rubbish. Work on changing yourself and leave me out of it.

Ikudayisi   No, I'm proud of who I am.

He sings.

> Green white green on my chest,
> I'm proud to be a Nigerian!
> Green white green on my chest,
> I'm proud to be a Nigerian!

Yemi   Oh my dayz!

Ikudayisi
> Green white green on my chest,
> I'm proud to be a Nigerian!

Yemi   Do you not see how stupid you look?

Ikudayisi
> Green white green on my chest,
> I'm proud to be a Nigerian!

He falls to his knees with his hands in the air.

> Proud to be a Nigerian,
> Proud to be a Nigerian,
> Proud – to – be – a – Ni-ge-ri-an,
> Proud – to – be – a – Ni-ge-ri-an!

Yemi   But then you put on a fake American accent when you talking to other people.

Ikudayisi *stops singing.*

Ikudayisi   That is just my accent, it is always changing.

Yemi   No. (*He mimics* **Ikudayisi***'s accent.*) This is your accent. (*He mimics* **Ikudayisi***'s fake American accent.*) And this is you when you're trying to be American. They are two different accents.

Ikudayisi   I'm still proud to be Nigerian.

Yemi   You're telling me I'm lost, but what bout you? You can stand here all day going on bout how proud you are, but the truth is in your action, not just your word.

Ikudayisi   Jo, leave me.

Yemi   Ohh, did I hit a raw nerve? Don't worry – as I said, your accent a joke, everyone understands why you want to get rid. It's no big ting. No one ain't gonna hate you if you change – I've already told you, I think you need to!

Ikudayisi   You are so young, you don't understand anything at all. I was once like you. As I keep on saying, I just wish you went to Nigeria. The way you are talking you will see –

Yemi   I don't *wanna* go there.

Ikudayisi   That's your problem, and why I personally feel sorry for you. You are telling me I need to change, but I'm not the one with the problem, it's you. You are a lost puppy. One minute you feel you don't fit in here because people are racist but then you don't want to be a Nigerian. Then you want to be left alone, but you complain you have no friend. Do you know who you are, Yemi?

Yemi   Yes, I'm a free person.

Ikudayisi   Nobody is free-oh.

Yemi   You might not be, but I am.

Ikudayisi   How can you be free when you deny your own heritage? You don't like your name, you are ashamed of your language. If you are *so* free you won't care what people think about Nigerian and you will just be what you are.

Yemi   Do you think I care what people think? It's not other people that make me hate Nigeria, it's Nigeria that makes me hate it.

Ikudayisi   *But you have never been there*. How can you judge? Nigeria is a nice place.

Yemi   Forget it, man. You're not going to make me change my mind overnight. Let's go.

Ikudayisi   No, ah ah.

Yemi   I don't give a shit bout Nigeria. Why can't you just leave it?

Ikudayisi   YOU NEED TO LEARN TO RESPECT IT! What are you going to teach your children?

Yemi   THAT THEY ARE FREE LIKE ME.

Ikudayisi   And when they want to know about their family?

Yemi   This is long, man, lauw da chat.

Ikudayisi   No. Will you even give your kids Yoruba names?

Yemi   I don't care.

Ikudayisi   WELL, YOU SHOULD!

Yemi   Why? Why should I? I'm not you, I'm my own person. Stop trying to force your views on me. I'm sick of this. I just wanna be me. Don't wanna be no one else. Let me be me. Why do you care what I think?

Ikudayisi   You *really* don't understand. Despite all its problem, Nigeria is a great place. YOU HAVE TO BE PROUD OF WHERE YOU ARE FROM.

Yemi   If it's so great, why do you *all* wanna come here?

Ikudayisi *remains silent.*

Yemi   *Exactly!* No matter how bad this country is, I bet it better than there!

Ikudayisi   *Ironi yen.* [A lie.]

Yemi *cuts his eye at* **Ikudayisi** *and kisses his teeth.*

Ikudayisi   I don't understand you at all. If people saw us now they would not even know we are from the same mother.

We are brothers, and you act like we are from different countries, different worlds.

Yemi   We are.

Blackout.

Scene Seven

It is early evening, and **Yemi** *and* **Ikudayisi** *are still out on the estate. They have finally got the milk and are heading home. They have been to a chicken-and-chips shop, too, and are eating on the way.*

Yemi *spots* **Blazer** *and pushes* **Ikudayisi** *behind him so it looks like they are not walking together. He quickens his pace and tries to act cool.*

Blazer   What's up, blud?

Yemi   I'm cool, man.

Ikudayisi *(in dodgy American accent)* Yeah, what's poppin?

Yemi   AHHH, MAN!

He gives **Ikudayisi** *a dirty look.* **Blazer** *laughs.*

Blazer   Who is dis?

Yemi   Erm . . .

Ikudayisi *(dodgy American accent)*   His older brother.

Blazer   I never knew you had a brother.

Yemi   I wish I never.

Blazer   What?

Yemi   Long story – he just come from Nigeria.

Blazer *(to* **Ikudayisi***)   Ba wo ni.* [Hi.]

Yemi   What?

Ikudayisi *(goes to nudge* **Blazer***)   Fellow Nigerian, how now?

Yemi   You're Nigerian? I thought –

Blazer   Course I'm Nigerian – one hundred per cent. (*To*
Ikudayisi.) *Se en gbadun ilu oyinbo?* [Are you enjoying England?]

Ikudayisi   *Ko bad now.* [Not bad.]

Yemi   What you two saying?

Blazer   Don't you understand Yoruba?

Yemi   No.

Ikudayisi   *Ko gbo nkan nkan.* [He doesn't understand anything.]

Blazer (*to* **Ikudayisi**)   Why ain't you teaching him?

Ikudayisi   I've tried-oh.

Yemi   Tried what?

Ikudayisi   To teach you Yoruba. (*To* **Blazer**.) But he said he
don't give a shit about Nigeria, he telling me I need to change,
forget about my heritage, be *free* like him.

Blazer (*to* **Yemi**)   Did you say dat?

Yemi   Nah, I never.

Ikudayisi   *Iro ti fo ori e.* [Lies are filled in his head.]

Blazer *laughs.*

Yemi   What did he say?

Blazer   Dat's why you need to learn to speak Yoruba, you
nah.

Yemi   Uhhh.

Blazer   So dat you know what people are saying bout you.

Yemi   True dat, true dat. I never thought of it like dat.

Ikudayisi   What! True what? (*To* **Blazer**.) Before he was
saying dat he don't want to have anything to do with Nigeria.
He was talking nonsense, saying dat he is free, dat we are from
different worlds.

Yemi   So? He tries to act like he is American.

Blazer   You *both* got something to learn.

Ikudayisi   I'm one hundred per cent proud of being Nigerian.

Yemi   Ehh, you think you're American.

Blazer (*to* **Ikudayisi**)   Blud, what is that all about?

Ikudayisi   When I put on the accent I'm only playing. I know who I am and where I'm from.

Blazer   Good, cos that LA Lagos shit pisses me off.

Yemi   Me too.

Ikudayisi   Me too what? You still don't know yourself.

Yemi   Shut up, man, you're chatting shit.

Blazer   Don't talk to your brother like dat, man. I swear he said he is older than you.

Yemi   So?

Blazer   So you need to learn to respect him, you nah. You can't go around talking to him like that. That's what makes us different.

Yemi   What does?

Blazer   Respect.

Yemi   From who?

Blazer   Da West Indians.

Yemi   See, that what I was trying to tell Dayisi bout us being different –

Ikudayisi   You were not talking about respect, you were talking rubbish.

Yemi   No I wasn't, I was saying –

Blazer   You two should know this already. Respect is something you shouldn't play wid. My mum taught me that years ago.

He begins to sing.

Money, power, respect is what you need in life.

Yemi *joins in.*

Yemi
Money, power, respect is the key to life.
You see in life, it's your given right.

Blazer   See, you know the song.

Yemi   Course, blud!

Blazer   Every word is the truth, mate.

Pause.

You see me, yeah, on the street I get bare respect, but don't get it twisted, it never came easy. I had to earn that shit. From when I learnt at home to show my family respect I came out on the road and showed mans respect. It like a chain reaction. You give respect to get respect, you get me?

Yemi   Yeah, man, I understand.

Ikudayisi   Hey-oh. God is listening to my prayers. (*To* **Yemi**.) You need more friends like this-oh.

Yemi   Shut –

Blazer   Yemi! I thought you understood. Come on, man, you couldn't have just forgotten what I *just* said.

Yemi   Sorry.

Blazer   It's important for you to respect him, man. He your older brother.

Yemi   I'm gonna try.

Blazer   It's not bout trying, you got to. He gonna show you tings no one can teach you.

Yemi   Nah, blud, *I'm* da one that teaching him tings.

Ikudayisi   It's a lie.

Blazer   If you were in Nigeria you would be calling him uncle, you nah.

Yemi   What?

Ikudayisi   It's true-oh.

Yemi   I'm not sure bout dat one – he is not my uncle, he is my brother.

Ikudayisi   You should even be bowing down to me.

Yemi   Please!

Blazer   He right. Even *now* I don't call my sister by her name and she is only two years older than me. I call her auntie.

Yemi   Even in the street?

Blazer   The streets, at home, everywhere. *Blud*, I don't play when it comes to being respectful, you nah.

Yemi   Don't you care what people think?

Blazer   Fuck what people think. You think I care? What da fuck can they try say to me? I'll have up any mans if they try to disrespect my tradition.

Pause.

You see me, yeah. I ain't ashamed of nothing.

Pause.

When I was younger, people used to take the piss out of me cos I had an accent. And it used to get me *mad*, but I never used to say nothing. But then one day I had enough and every man who tried to take the piss – got knocked out. Straight!

Yemi   I remember hearing your fight stories, but I never knew the reasons behind it. You kept it real, blud.

Blazer   So what, you think now people will try take the piss with me now?

Yemi   No.

Blazer   Exactly. It's not going to happen. They can say what they want behind my back, but to my face, mans have to be careful what they say. And that's the way I like it. Gone are da days when mans take the piss out of this African! Cos I run this estate now. And you know, I know they don't like it. But what can they do? The roles have reversed now.

Yemi   Rahh, I like it! I like it.

Blazer   I'm not saying to you, go around testing people. You just need to learn how to stand your ground, but keep it real at the same time. It's not a bad thing to be African. Be proud to be different.

Yemi   I will man . . . I mean, I am.

Blazer   Make sure you start to learn Yoruba from your brother.

Yemi   Yeah, course.

Blazer (*to* **Ikudayisi**)   Make sure you teach him.

Ikudayisi   *Mo gbo.* [I understand.]

Blazer (*to* **Yemi**)   Even if you want, blud, come round to mines, I will teach you. It's easy once you get started. (*To* **Ikudayisi**.) And make sure you don't put on that fake accent again.

Ikudayisi (*in dodgy American accent*))   No problem.

Blazer   Oi.

Ikudayisi   I told you, it was joke I'm playing, I'm playing –

Blazer (*to* **Yemi**)   What's your full name?

Yemi   Oluyemi Adewale.

Blazer   Do you know what it means?

Yemi   Nah.

Ikudayisi   I know.

Yemi   Tell me.

Blazer   Don't tell him. Let him find it out himself – it would be a good lesson for him. That's your first assignment.

Yemi   Why? What does it mean?

Blazer   It's your mission. You need to investigate it yourself.

Yemi   OK.

Pause.

Blazer   So what's this I'm hearing bout some mad run-in with Armani?

Yemi   How do you know? . . . I never done nothing to her – is that why you come to chat to me?

Blazer   No, calm down, Yemi man, it's a question.

Yemi   Oh, she is just a fool who talks too much.

Blazer   You don't got to say that twice.

Yemi   So how did you know about my run-in with her?

Blazer   I heard her telling Razer.

Yemi   So, what, he's proper looking for me now? Man ready for war, you nah?

Blazer   Nah, blud, calm down. They weren't even paying attention to her anyways.

Yemi   *Dey?*

Blazer   You know, Razer and Flamer are always together.

Yemi   So dey must be looking for me den.

Blazer   Nah, man, don't worry.

Yemi   I'm not. I telling you, I'm ready for dem mans if they wanna start something.

Blazer   Calm down. So for the last ten minutes you ain't heard a word I said.

Yemi   I did – you said to stand your ground.

Blazer   When needed!

Pause.

Dem youth are my soldier, man. They can't make any
movement without my say so. I don't want you to get into no
madness. I will talk to dem if you want.

Yemi   If mans come, I just know to be prepared, innit.

Blazer   Stop talking like dat, man. You got to pick your
battles wise, you know. Look, I'm having a word with dem.
You're too young to be getting into madness.

Yemi   Nah, it cool.

Blazer   Seriously, I don't mind to chat to dem. Us Nigerians
need to stick together. (*To* **Ikudayisi**.) Innit.

Ikudayisi   Of course now.

Yemi   It cool.

Blazer   OK. But don't do nothing stupid. One.

He nudges **Yemi** *and* **Ikudayisi** *and exits.*

Ikudayisi   I like him-oh.

Yemi *stares after* **Blazer**.

Ikudayisi   I said dat I think he is a cool guy.

Yemi *still ignores him.*

Ikudayisi   YEMI, are you listening?

Yemi   WHAT?

Ikudayisi   Your friend, he is a cool guy.

Yemi   Yeah, he is alright.

Ikudayisi   What wrong now?

Yemi   Nothing. I can't believe he is Nigerian. I can see it now
but I never saw it before.

Pause.

Do you know, that the first time he has ever proper stopped and chat to me? Usually it's just hi and bye.

Ikudayisi   And so?

Yemi   Don't you think it's strange with all that been happening today?

Ikudayisi   Stop over-analysing everything. Did you not hear a word he was saying?

Yemi *is still looking into the distance.*

Ikudayisi   Yemi, you are reading too much into it.

Yemi *is still silent.*

Ikudayisi   Snap out of it.

Ikudayisi *clicks his fingers in front of* **Yemi***'s face.*

Yemi   What does my name mean?

Ikudayisi   Now you want to learn.

Yemi   Stop being silly, just tell me.

Ikudayisi   Give me a hundred pound, and I'll tell you.

Yemi   Yeah, right! Just tell me, man.

Ikudayisi   OK, fifty pounds.

Yemi   This is why you get on my nerves.

Ikudayisi   OK, OK . . . it means 'God suit you'.

Yemi   'God suits me'! That's crap, man.

Ikudayisi   No, I mean, it hard to change it from Yoruba to English. It is better in Yoruba. Oluyemi is a big name.

Yemi   Whatever. Why did he go on like it was important for me to find out? What was he talking bout I need to know what it mean? That don't mean shit.

Ikudayisi   Nigerians believes names hold power.

Yemi   Why?

Ikudayisi   Cos they think that people will live up to it, they have special meaning.

Yemi   What does your name mean?

Ikudayisi   'Death spared me'.

Yemi   WHAT?! I should have got that name.

Ikudayisi   I came first.

Yemi   But that type of name don't suit you. You ain't no warrior. It suits a fighter like me!

Ikudayisi   Dat not what it means.

Yemi   What does it mean then, if it's not a warrior name?

Ikudayisi   It means that when Mum was having me she may have had some complications – you know, cos she had me young, and death spared me. I survived!

Yemi   *I don't care*, I should have had that name.

Ikudayisi   Look at you – now you want a Nigerian name. Anyway, I'm happy-oh.
  Green white green on my chest,
  You're proud to be a Nigerian.

Ikudayisi *starts to sing his song and notices* **Yemi** *bounces his head.*

Ikudayisi   Eh, eh, so now you are proud.

Yemi *pushes* **Ikudayisi**.

Yemi   Move. Shut up, man!

They begin to play-fight and **Yemi** *gets* **Ikudayisi** *in a head lock.*

Yemi   You may be older than me, but I'm stronger. See, that why I should have had your name.

Ikudayisi   Let go of me.

Yemi   Who's your daddy?

Ikudayisi   Olakunle Adewale.

Yemi   No, you fool, say I'm your dad.

Ikudayisi   No.

Yemi   Say it and I'll let go.

Ikudayisi   No.

Yemi   Who's your dad?

Ikudayisi   You are squeezing my neck. I can't breathe.

Yemi   Say I'm your dad and I'll let go.

Ikudayisi   I can't breathe!

Two **Police Officers** *come onto the estate.*

Police Officer 1   Oi, can I have word with you?

Yemi *lets go of* **Ikudayisi** *as* **Police Officer 1** *walks up to him.*
Ikudayisi *begins rubbing his neck.*

Ikudayisi (*to* **Yemi**)   You play too ruff, you dey hurt my neck-oh.

Police Officer 2 (*to* **Ikudayisi**)   You OK, son?

Yemi   Course he alright.

Police Officer 2   You will get your chance to speak in a minute, mate.

Yemi   We were just playing.

Police Officer 2   That's what they all say.

Yemi   What's that suppose to mean?

Police Officer 1   Watch your mouth, lad!

Yemi   What?

Ikudayisi   It's true, we were just playing.

Police Officer 2 *moves* **Ikudayisi** *away from* **Yemi**.

Police Officer 2 (*to* **Ikudayisi**)   Don't worry. We're here now, you ain't got to be scared anymore. Are you OK?

Ikudayisi   I'm OK . . .

Yemi   I told you we were just playing.

Police Officer 2   And I said *that's* what they all say.

Yemi   Are you buzzing, blud? What's your beef?

Police Officer 2   Who do you think you're talking to? I ain't your pal or your mate. Does it look like we are from the same blood? Show some respect and talk properly.

Yemi *heads to confront* **Police Officer 2** *but* **Police Officer 1** *gets in the way and they both crowd over him.*

Yemi   Man is speaking English.

Police Officer 2   You're not a man, you're still a boy.

Police Officer 1 (*to* **Yemi**)   So where you heading off to now?

Yemi *remains silent.*

Police Officer 1   You deaf, *boy*? I'm asking you a question.

Yemi *still remains silent.*

Police Officer 1 (*holds* **Yemi***'s face*) I said, *where* are you going?

Yemi   NOWHERE. I ain't got to speak to you if I don't want to.

Police Officer 1   Do you wanna be answering these questions at a police station? If not, start talking.

Yemi   Is there something you're looking for?

Police Officer 2   Is there something *you're* tryna hide?

Yemi   You got time on your hands. I know my right. Why don't you go and fight real crime.

Police Officer 1   Black-on-black violence *is* a crime.

Police Officer 2 *laughs.*

Ikudayisi   Please, what's the problem, sir?

Police Officer 1   We're just trying to find out what the problem is here, son.

Yemi   There is no problem – we were playing. Mans like you is just tryna harass us.

Police Officer 2 (*to* **Police Officer 1**)   You understand what he saying?

Police Officer 1   Kids find it so hard to speak English nowadays.

Police Officer 2   All that seems to come out their mouths is bumba clat this, bumba clat that, and innit man, yeah man.

Police Officer 1   Such a disgrace. Schools really ain't teaching them anything.

Police Officer 2   I think I should start up my own school.

Police Officer 1   Oh yeah, what would you call it?

Yemi   You two are nuts. Let's go, Dayisi.

Yemi *begins to walk around them and* **Police Officer 2** *grabs his hand.*

Yemi   Let go of my hand.

Police Officer 1   We have not finished here.

Yemi   Man, best let go.

Police Officer 1   *Oohh*, is that a threat?

Police Officer 2   Sounds like one to me. You getting ready to assault a police officer?

Yemi   You don't know me – when I make a threat, *you will know*!

Police Officer 2   Oohh, I think the Yardie is getting mad.

Police Officer 1 (*in a dodgy Jamaican accent*)   Bumba clat, we may need some backup, man, up in de place.

Police Officer 2   And request for the drug squad.

Police Officer 1 (*in a dodgy Jamaican accent*)   SO man may start shooting up de place, he na care, him gangsta.

The two **Police Officers** *begin to laugh at their own jokes while* **Yemi** *still struggles.*

Yemi   Shows how much you know. I'm not even Jamaican. I'm Nigerian.

Police Officer 1   Stop being silly, you're not from Africa, he is.

Ikudayisi   We're both Nigerian.

Police Officer 2   He don't act African. He lied to you, son, he is a Jamaican.

Yemi   Yeah, I am Nigerian.

Police Officer 2   Let me see your passport.

Police Officer 1   You mean his photocopy?

Yemi (*to* **Ikudayisi**)   You hearing this now. I told you they treat you different when you are black.

Ikudayisi   Yemi, shh.

Yemi   What? Why should I be quiet, you blind?

Ikudayisi   Please, sir, we are just coming from de shop.

Police Officer 1   Don't worry, we know how to deal with him. We handle situations like this on a daily basis.

Yemi *still struggles with* **Police Officer 2** *but his grip on him gets tighter.*

Yemi   Stop tryna take the fucking piss.

Police Officer 2   Watch your language, son.

Yemi   I ain't your son.

Police Officer 2   Glad you ain't. If I had a child I'd teach him to have a lot more respect than you.

Yemi   Look – what do you want?

Police Officer 1   For you to show some manners and respect.

Yemi   But I'm not even doing nothing.

Police Officer 2   You're causing a scene.

Yemi   You're the one's who is *harassing* me. Touching me for no reason. You know you ain't got nothing on us. (*He gets free. To* **Ikudayisi**.) Let's go!

Police Officer 2   He is not going anywhere with you.

Yemi *attempts to grab* **Ikudayisi**'s *hand.* **Police Officer 1** *holds him back again.*

Yemi   STOP TRYNA FUCKING TOUCH ME UP. YOU BATTY MAN!

Police Officer 1   Ohh, bad mistake!

He starts to bring out the handcuffs.

Ikudayisi   Please, sir, he doesn't mean it.

Police Officer 2   Just stand over here, son.

Yemi   You can't hold me against my will.

Police Officer 1   We can if we suspect you being under the influence.

Yemi   Under the influence of what?

Police Officers 1 *and* **2**   Cannabis.

Yemi   Dat's how I know you're chatting shit. Can you even smell anything on me?

Ikudayisi   Sir, please, how much do you want.

He begins searching in his pockets.

Yemi (*to* **Ikudayisi**)   Dayisi, are you mad, you don't got to pay for nothing.

Ikudayisi   How much do you want? I will go and get it and you can let him go.

Yemi   Stop talking!

Police Officer 2 (*to* **Ikudayisi**)   Son, we're not corrupt officers, we don't take bribes – just sorting out this little dispute for you, OK?

Ikudayisi   Please, we don't want trouble.

Police Officer 2 (*to* **Ikudayisi**)   Don't worry, it's not you that's causing the problems. (*He gets out his notebook. To* **Yemi**.) We will try this again. What is your name?

Yemi   I really ain't got time for this. Arrest me, innit.

Police Officer 1   Well, disturbing the peace is a big offence.

Yemi   Disturbing the peace, disturbing the peace – you're disturbing *my* peace. You came up to me with nothing to say, nothing! Just tryna force me to get mad. TO GET MAD SO I WILL DO SOMETHING, SO YOU CAN DO ME FOR SOMINK. That's how I know you people are corrupt. When you should be out doing something constructive. You're bugging me cos I'm black.

Police Officer 1   Don't try and use the race card here, boy, and keep your voice down.

Police Officer 2   There is nothing racist about us, stop tryna make a scene.

Yemi   You're stopping me from going home.

Police Officer 1   Home?

Police Officer 2   If you were willing to say that in the first place, of course we would have let you go home. Go on then.

Yemi   What?

Ikudayisi   We are sorry, sir.

Yemi   SHUT UP, DAYISI, WHAT YOU SAYING SORRY FOR? These mans are taking us for dickhead. Are you blind?

Yemi *goes to push him and the* **Police Officers** *hold him back.*

Yemi   The only reason they acting nice now is cos there are bare people around, looking at them, knowing they are being racist!

Police Officer 1   Oi, leave him alone.

Police Officer 2 (*to onlookers*)   This is why, people, we're here. Just looking out for *his* best interest. (*To* **Ikudayisi**.) We wouldn't want anything to happen to you whilst you're in this country.

Ikudayisi   Uh?

Yemi (*to* **Ikudayisi**)   This is what I've been telling you all day, all day, but you never wanted to listen to me. What did I tell you bout this country?

Police Officer 2   Stop causing a scene.

Yemi   Nah, people need to hear what's going on.

Police Officer 1   Stop trying to be a smart alec.

Yemi (*begins shouting while being held*)   The only reason why these mans are holding me is cos I'm black. I ain't done nothing and they tryna arrest me.

A message comes in on the police radio about a more important case.

I'm being harassed, I'm being harassed!

Police Officer 2   Today's your lucky day, son.

Yemi *and* **Ikudayisi** *start to move, but get stopped again.*

Police Officer 1   No, you go that way and we will help him out.

Yemi   But we live *that* way.

Police Officer 2   There is still a chance of you getting arrested.

Ikudayisi   Please, he is my brother, sir.

Police Officer 1   You don't have to *pretend*, son, he won't trouble you again.

Yemi *kisses his teeth and heads off to the right. The* **Police Officers** *stay and watch till he goes offstage.*

Police Officer 1   Off you go then.

Ikudayisi But –

Police Officer 2   Don't worry, son, we got you covered.

The **Police Officers** *stay and watch as* **Ikudayisi** *walks off to the left. He glances backwards once or twice, but the* **Police Officers** *stand their ground till he is out of sight.*

Blackout.

Scene Eight

On the other side of the estate, **Razer** *and* **Armani** *are walking down the street.* **Razer** *has his arms around* **Armani**.

Razer   You need to be more nicer to your friend, you nah.

Armani   Uh.

Razer   Paris, man, she is the only friend you got.

Armani   What? Whose side are you on? You saw the way she tried to speak to me.

Razer   Ah, don't worry. You two will be talking by the end of tonight.

Armani   I won't. She gets on my nerves and I'll let her know dat. I'm not fake – if I don't like someone I make dem know.

Razer   She's cool, man. How come she ain't got a boyfriend?

Armani   Cos she ugly.

Razer   Stop being silly. I'm tryna be serious.

Armani   Why are you interested for?

Razer   I'm not, it's for Flamer.

Armani   So let Flamer find out for himself. I'm never talking to her again.

Razer   You kinda messed up his flow.

Armani   How?

Razer   By making her storm off.

Armani   He needs to forget bout dat then.

Razer   Why?

Armani   Cos she tried to take me for an eediate, and I ain't no fool, and we are no longer friends.

Razer *lets go of* **Armani**.

Razer   You're so childish.

Armani   No, I'm just real.

Razer   No, you're just silly.

Armani   I don't know why you care. She is frigid, man. Anyways, Flamer don't stand a chance.

Razer   You're a hater, do you know that, Armani?

Armani   *No*, I'm not.

Razer   You are.

Armani   WHY ARE YOU SO FOCUSED ON TALKING BOUT PARIS FOR?

Razer   Forget it. Sometimes you get on my nerves. Man can't even have a civilised conversation with you without you running up your mouth.

Armani   I'm sorry. It's just today been a mad day. Everyone is trying to have a go at me. This is suppose to be a free country and people are not even allowing me to speak my mind.

Razer   Don't take it out on me.

Armani   Paris never even had my back.

Razer   You told this story already.

Armani   And you're my man, so don't you think you should have stood up for me when that dickhead African Blazer was shouting at me?

Razer   If you kept quiet Blazer would have left you.

Armani   And even when Paris tried to tell all those lies you never even said anything.

Razer   Aaaah, man.

Armani   Its true, dough – you could have said something.

Razer   Armani, you started most of these argument. What do you expect me to say?

Pause.

Armani   You gonna sort that Yemi out den?

Razer   Why?

Armani   Because these Africans are forgetting their place and you need to show him.

Razer   I'm not involved in this African war ting you're tryna start.

Armani   But he tried to attack me.

Razer   So? You tryna say you never done nothing to provoke him?

Armani   No – you know Africans are animals, man. He just went mad on me. He hit me in the head and he called you a dickhead, saying you can't do shit to him. You can't let him get away wid dat.

Razer   I'm not troubling nobody. If I get in trouble one more time I'm getting locked down, and I ain't going jail for no chick.

Armani   But –

Razer   Listen! I told you I'm not getting locked down for stupidness. Didn't you hear anything I said before? No chick gonna be the reason I get locked up, including you, Armani.

Armani   Then maybe you shouldn't be my man. I need a man who can look after me, one who is not afraid.

Razer   Go then.

Armani   A man is supposed to look out for his girl – he is
meant to protect her no matter what.

Razer   I said, go then. Go fine a man better dan me.

Armani   That's why I should have gone out with Flamer.
He's is not afraid of no one.

Razer   FUCK OFF!

Armani   You don't have to be so rude. What's your problem?

Razer   WHAT IS YOURS? You giving me a headache, man.
I'm telling you to stop talking and all you do is talk. Can't you
just be quiet for once, man? That's what gets you into trouble
– your mouth. And you want me to get involved in your
bullshit. I only fight battles that worth fighting. I'm tryna make
changes and you're tryna force me to go down the wrong road.

Armani   Are you on your period or something?

Razer   Piss off, man.

Razer *puts up his hood and walks off, leaving* **Armani** *speechless.*

Blackout.

Scene Nine

It is now around eight in the evening, and **Flamer** *is walking on the
estate by himself when* **Ikudayisi** *runs onstage.*

Ikudayisi   YEMI, YEMI, WHERE ARE YOU NOW?

He bumps into **Flamer**.

Flamer   You idiot.

Ikudayisi   I'm sorry-oh, I didn't see you.

Flamer   So, what, I'm too black now?

Ikudayisi   Don't be stupid.

Flamer   You calling me stupid?

Ikudayisi   No, you don't understand. I'm saying how can I not see you, you are not that black.

Flamer *looks down at his trainers and sees one has a mark on it.*

Flamer   Look at my trainer, blud. Are you on a hype ting?

Ikudayisi   I'm sorry.

Flamer   What, is *that* all you're gonna say?

Ikudayisi   What do you want me to say now? It was only an accident. I didn't mean it.

Flamer   So what you gonna do about it then?

Ikudayisi   What do you want me to do? You can go home and clean it.

Flamer   Blud, do you think I'm a dickhead?

Ikudayisi   Please, I don' have time for this, I have to look for my brother.

Ikudayisi *start to walk off but* **Flamer** *catches hold of him.*

Flamer   Did I say we have finish?

Ikudayisi   What is wrong with today-oh? Why is everyone stopping people from walking? All I want to do is go home. I have said I'm sorry. What else do you want me to do?

Flamer   Sorry ain't gonna pay for it. I want my fifty pound!

Ikudayisi   Fifty pound for dis dirty trainer. Kayi! I don't have that kind of money-oh.

Flamer   Is this man dizzy? You steps on my foot and now you're tryna take me for an eediate. Are you buzzing?

Ikudayisi   I beg your pardon? I don't understand what you just said.

Flamer   What? All of a sudden you don't understand English now? Man better start understanding what I'm saying.

Flamer *brings out a knife.*

Ikudayisi   Ahhh, ARMED ROBBER! (*He raises his hands in the air.*) Be careful-oh. *Jo ma pa me! Ma pa me-oh!* [Don't kill me.]

Flamer   Speak English.

Ikudayisi   I don't have anything on me – please don't kill me.

Flamer   I'm not playing around! Give me my money.

Ikudayisi   I beg-oh. I don't have no money with me.

Flamer   Empty out your pockets.

Ikudayisi   Ah ah, now you don't believe me. Why will I lie? Look, I live on this estate. Give me your trainer and I will go and wash it for you now.

Flamer   I have never seen you round here before, so don't take me for an eediate. Empty your pocket.

Ikudayisi *empties out his pockets.*

Flamer   Where is your phone?

Ikudayisi   I don't have one.

Flamer   You ain't got a phone? What type of . . . ?

He looks **Ikudayisi** *up and down from head to toe.*

Flamer   Take off your trainers.

Ikudayisi   Ah, ah, I can't give you the trainers, I said I will clean your shoe for you.

Flamer   I said, take off the trainers.

Ikudayisi   It's not mine. Please, it's my brother's.

Flamer   Take off the fucking trainer, now.

Ikudayisi   Please, I didn't mean to step on your trainer. It was an accident, ah ah –

Flamer *moves closer to* **Ikudayisi** *with the knife.* **Ikudayisi** *quickly takes off the trainers.*

Ikudayisi   What is happening to this country? Why are you behaving like dis?

Yemi *enters and sees what is happening. He shouts over.*

Yemi   Oi!

Flamer *takes the trainers and runs.* **Yemi** *runs over to* **Ikudayisi**.

Yemi   Why you letting people push you around? This is what I mean bout you need to change.

Ikudayisi   Just leave me. *Awon olori buruku.* [These horrible people.]

Yemi   What happen, man?

Ikudayisi   This London *babanla problem lo wa fumi* [This London is nothing but trouble for me.]

Yemi   I don't have time for this – what happen?

Pause.

Where is your – I mean *my* trainers?

Ikudayisi   He took it now.

Yemi   You got *jacked*!

Ikudayisi   No!

Yemi   So what happened?

Ikudayisi   I stepped on his trainer –

Yemi   You let someone take your trainers and you never even fought back? What the hell is wrong with you? See, see, I thought everyone was nice to you! You just made a man take you for an eediate and you couldn't do nothing.

Ikudayisi   I tried now.

Yemi   Tried! Tried! I swear in African you train with lion.

Ikudayisi   Yemi, don't start that . . . In Nigeria people die over things like this all the time-oh. I value my life. He had a knife.

Yemi   So?

Ikudayisi   What did you want me to do?

Yemi   NOT TO GET ROBBED!

Ikudayisi   I said he had a knife.

Yemi   If that was me, I would fight him same way. Do you think I care? You just made a man take you for an eediate and you didn't do nothing? And you were saying I don't know what I'm talking bout. I DON'T KNOW WHAT I'M TALKING ABOUT! Do you *now* see what this country is like? Do you see?

Ikudayisi   Where were you, eh?

Yemi   What! You tryna switch this on me? Was you not there when the police told me to walk? If you had any sense you would have followed me, instead of just standing around with them.

Ikudayisi   They told me to wait.

Yemi   Why did you listen?

Ikudayisi   Why didn't you stay?

Yemi   So is it my fault? You're a big boy and you got rob – I would never let that happen to me.

Ikudayisi   It wasn't my fault, it wasn't my fault. I beg him not to take it, he didn't listen. I'm not going to get killed because of trainer.

Yemi   You pussy.

Ikudayisi   I don't like this country. *Babalan* [enormous] problem.

Armani *enters, looking for* **Razer**.

Armani   Razer, where are you? RAZER!

She sees **Yemi**, *cuts her eye at him, then quickly runs off the other way.*

Yemi   Come on, let's go.

Ikudayisi   Where are you going to go?

Yemi   I'm going to settle this once and for all.

Ikudayisi   I don't have shoes on.

Yemi   We are going after the shoes.

Ikudayisi   You don't know where it is.

Yemi   Do you think it a coincidence that that girl is looking for her man in the same place you got robbed? Open your eyes.

Ikudayisi   Who?

Yemi   Armani. You blind? Did you not just see her come round da corner?

Ikudayisi   I don't want trouble. Let's just go home. We already have the milk. Mum will be worried.

Yemi   In this country you ain't got to look for trouble before it finds you. Can you not see dat? If you don't go for what is yours, they will always think you're a dickhead. If you don't stand your ground.

Ikudayisi   Who?

Yemi   Dem. That crew, it was dat Armani chick that told dem to come for you. We need to show them that they can't take us for eediate.

Ikudayisi   Please, let's just go home.

Yemi   Didn't you hear what Blazer was saying before?

Ikudayisi   Oh, please, eh, I don't like this.

Yemi ˙ He said, yeah, we have to demand respect. I'm going to teach you how to stand your ground.

Ikudayisi   Listen to me, Yemi, I'm standing my ground now. Going after somebody who has a weapon is not good-oh. Yemi, I don't want to be a part of this. Let's go home.

Yemi   I ain't going nowhere till I sort this out. I have let this go on for too many years now. Mans ain't gonna take me for a dickhead *no more*!

Ikudayisi   Forget about years ago. You have to learn to choose your battle. There are more important things to fight over. Believe me.

Yemi   *Yes*, and this is one of them.

Ikudayisi   No, it's not – please, look, this is why you need to go to Nigeria and see. Things like this is small, small.

Yemi   Shut up! *Shut up!* Now is not the time to start talking your Nigerian shit.

Ikudayisi   Then what is it you are going to fight for? You are running to go and prove a point, but you don't know what point you are making.

Yemi   I'm doing this for me. I'm gonna make people know who I am.

Ikudayisi   Please, Yemi, this is not a good idea.

Yemi   Move out my way, Dayisi.

Ikudayisi   No, I can't let you do this. You have been telling me all day I need to change, but now it's time for you to stop and think. You make me laugh, you go on like your life is so hard. Believe me, you have it easy. Once you stop thinking dat the whole world has declared war on you, you will see how great your life is.

Yemi   Why don't you care about the fact that you just got robbed?

Ikudayisi   I told, I told you, it's not important. Do you think I have never had to make choices? I told you I was once like you. Is it the first time I got robbed? *No!* In Nigeria it happens all the time – even the police have robbed in broad daylight. I used to put up a fight but I told you, you soon realise thing like this is not important. As long as I'm alive, I'm happy. Friends in Nigerian have died over nonsense like this. I want to enjoy my life – those are the changes I have made. Don't waste your life away like this.

Yemi   Move. You ain't got to follow me,. You can go off home.

Ikudayisi *tries to hold him back.*

Yemi   Get off me. This is going to be sorted with or without you!

Blackout.

Scene Ten

Armani *has caught up with* **Razer** *and they are walking together when* **Yemi** *comes round the corner, followed by* **Ikudayisi**.

Yemi   Oi, RAZER! Yeah, you, I'm talking to you. Give me my shit back.

Razer (*looks stunned*)   What? (*To* **Armani**.) What's he talking bout?

Armani   Move, you dickhead, who do you think you're talking to like that?

Ikudayisi   It wasn't him.

Yemi   Blud, why are you tryna take man for a dickhead?

Razer   What? What's wrong wid you people?

Yemi   I want it back now.

Armani   Are you crazy? Go talk your gibberish elsewhere, man.

Yemi   You think it is a coincidence my brother got robbed five minutes ago and then the only people I see on road – is you two?

Razer   Your brother?

Yemi   Yes, my brother. Don't think I'm stupid. You messed with the wrong person now.

Razer   Shut up, man. Move.

Armani   YEAH, DUSS.

Yemi (*to* **Armani**)   You shut up.

Armani   That's what I'm saying, Razer. Look, he is tryna get rude. Put him in his place. You see I wasn't lying. Look how he is acting like an animal.

Razer   Blud, just go home. I'm not in the mood.

Razer *tries to walk off but* **Yemi** *holds him back.*

Ikudayisi   Yemi, I told you it wasn't him.

Yemi   Only mans like him like to take advantage of people who can't defend themselves.

Armani   Be quiet, you bubo.

Yemi   I will knock you out.

Ikudayisi   *Omo girl e.* [Oh this girl.] Shut up your mouth.

Armani   SPEAK ENGLISH.

Razer *moves towards* **Ikudayisi**.

Razer   Don't talk to my girl like dat.

Yemi   He will talk to her any way he wants. Don't try to take him for an eediate and think he will sit down bout it. Give me my shit back.

Razer   Blud, don't get rude.

Yemi   What, you think you can pick on him cos he is African, but you can't deal with me?

Razer   I'm being nice – go home.

Yemi   Give me my tings and I'll go.

Armani   Razer, you're good, why don't you just thump him in his mouth, maybe then he will start making sense.

Yemi *moves close to* **Armani**.

Yemi   Thump who?

Ikudayisi   Yemi, leave her, it's not worth it at all. (*To* **Razer**.) We don't want trouble.

Razer   He seems to be asking it for it dough. You need to speak to your brother, cos I don't know what he is talking about.

Ikudayisi *tries to move* **Yemi**.

Yemi   DON'T TOUCH ME! I'm doing this for you. If you let people treat you like shit they will walk over you all your life.

Ikudayisi   Stop lying to yourself – I have already told you I'm not asking for this.

Yemi *pushes* **Ikudayisi** *and moves to* **Razer**.

Yemi   I just want my tings back.

Razer   Don't try and start something you can't finish.

Yemi   What dat suppose to mean?

Razer   This is da last time I'm going to tell you to go home. Don't try and get too big for your boot. Lauw da hype ting.

Yemi (*moves real close to* **Razer**)   I'm not on no hype ting – I just want my FUCKING TRAINERS BACK!

Armani (*to* **Razer**)   Why are you letting him talk to you like dat? This boy is a waste, man. DO SOMETHING.

Yemi *goes for* **Razer** *and* **Razer** *pulls out a knife.*

Razer   LOOK, I TOLD YOU GO HOME. Why are you making me do this?

Ikudayisi   Oh God, oh . . .

Razer   I'm trying, yeah, I'm trying. I don't wanna do this.

Yemi   You're making me mad and I don't want to get mad.

Razer   I DON'T WANNA GET MAD EITHER. Now I've told you I don't know what you're talking bout. So leave. NOW!

Ikudayisi   Please put it down.

Yemi (*to* **Ikudayisi**) Stop BEGGING PEOPLE. (*To* **Razer**.) I ain't scared of you, bruv. If you're gonna wet me then wet me. But I don't care, I'm not going anywhere till you people understand I ain't a dickhead. I ain't a dickhead.

Ikudayisi Please, let's go.

Armani Just wet him up, man, he deserves it.

Razer Shut up Armani, man.

As **Razer** *gets distracted* **Yemi** *goes for the knife. They get into a scrap and* **Yemi** *gains control over it.*

Yemi Who is bad now, who bad now?

Ikudayisi Yemi, put it down, you going to hurt somebody. It wasn't him.

Armani Yeah, listen to your brother.

Yemi BE QUIET. YOU'RE ALWAYS FUCKING TALKING. Don't you know when to keep your mouth shut, uh? You really think you're bad, innit.

Armani No.

He waves the knife at her.

Razer Yemi, I swear – put it down.

Armani No, please!

Yemi See, you're scared now. I thought you were a bad girl. African this and African that. You're not better than me now, are you? Carry on running your mouth, see if you don't get wet.

Ikudayisi Why can't you listen to me? I keep telling you – what you are fighting for is not worth it.

Yemi Don't you get it? I don't care. These lots go on like they run this fucking estate. It about time people sees who really runs this estate. These jams think they are better dan us Africans. Dat we ain't shit. That's why they robbed you. It something they do all the time. They treat Africans like they are beneath them. I AIN'T BENEATH NO ONE.

Razer   Look, I'm tryna stay out of trouble, I ain't robbed no one in time.

Yemi   Well, you messed with the wrong person.

Ikudayisi   I didn't come from Nigeria to be a part of this. We are all BLACK! WE ARE ALL BLACK AND YOU ARE ACTING LIKE WE ARE ALL DIVIDED! It needs to stop now. We need to stop this nonsense. Why are we always fighting each other? Why can't we just get along? I just want everyone to get along. Yemi, you tell me you are free, be free to make the right choice. Don't go down the wrong road. It's your choice, make the right choice. GIVE ME THE KNIFE.

Ikudayisi *goes for the knife and struggles with* **Yemi**. *In the process the knife falls and* **Razer** *picks it up again.*

Yemi (*to* **Ikudayisi**)   Why do I bother listening to you – look what you done.

Ikudayisi   He doesn't want no trouble, he is going – leave him.

Razer *starts to walk.* **Yemi** *grabs him.* **Ikudayisi** *tries to stop him and as he gets in between his arm gets cut by the knife.*

Ikudayisi   Ahhhh!

He falls to the ground.

Yemi   IKU, IKU!

He grabs **Ikudayisi** *and holds him.*

Armani   Razer, look what you done, look what you done.

Razer   I didn't mean to, it was just in my hand. It wasn't my fault, it wasn't my fault. Ah fuck man! Yemi, it wasn't my fault.

Blackout.

Scene Eleven

Two weeks later. **Yemi** *and* **Ikudayisi** *are in their bedroom.*
Ikudayisi *is in traditional African attire and is struggling to put on his hat because his arm is in a sling.* **Yemi** *is putting the agbada over his head and is profiling in front of the mirror.*

Mum (*offstage, shouting*)   You two children, what is taking you so long? We were supposed to be at the party from seven o'clock. Look at the time now.

Ikudayisi *and* **Yemi**   I'M WAITING FOR HIM!

They point at each other, look and begin laughing.

Mum (*off*)   People already think I don't have any control of you, that I leave you to gallivant and act like animals. What are they going to be thinking when we show up late, eh? . . . People always tell me that I'm –

Ikudayisi   LUCKY TO HAVE BIG BOYS!

Yemi   We are coming, Mum.

Mum (*off*)   I'M ONLY GIVING YOU TEN MORE MINUTES!

Ikudayisi (*turns to* **Yemi**)   You're waiting for me? I've been ready for an hour now and I'm the one that is handicap.

Yemi   Stop rinsing that line, it's played out now.

Ikudayisi   I know, I know, I just like making you feel guilty.

Yemi   Badmind.

Ikudayisi   I will never forget the look on your face that day when you thought I died.

Yemi   It wasn't funny, you nah. My heart skipped a beat.

Ikudayisi   And that Razer, I've never seen two boys cry as much as you two.

Yemi   Why do you have to keep on telling the story like that?

Ikudayisi   Cos that is how it happened. Iku, Iku, don't die, don't die.

Yemi *punches him in the arm.*

Ikudayisi   Ow.

Yemi   Oh shit, oh shit. I'm sorry, I'm sorry.

Ikudayisi *(starts laughing)*   You are so gullible. At least I know you really love me.

Yemi   Shut up.

Ikudayisi   Come on, say it, you love me.

Yemi   Leave me.

Ikudayisi   Not until you say you love me.

Yemi   No! Stop acting gay.

Ikudayisi   Just say it.

Yemi   No.

Ikudayisi   I can't hear you.

Yemi   Cos I never said it.

Ikudayisi   Why are you being so –

Mum *(off)*   YOU THESE CHILDREN, I HAVE BEEN NICE TO YOU SINCE THAT DAY – OH, BUT I WILL STOP BEING NICE IF YOU DON'T LISTEN.

Ikudayisi   *Mon bo, Ma.* [I'm coming, Mum.] *(To* **Yemi***.)* Just hurry up before she starts breathing fire and smoke comes out her nose.

Yemi   Yeah, OK.

Ikudayisi *turns to leave.*

Yemi   Ikudayisi.

Ikudayisi   Yeah?

Yemi   You have forgiven me, right?

Ikudayisi   For what?

He turns to leave again.

Yemi   Dayisi.

Ikudayisi   Yes?

Yemi   I'm sorry.

Ikudayisi   I know, I guess you now know what's important, right?

Yemi   Yeah, yeah I do.

Ikudayisi *goes to give* **Yemi** *a hug.*

Ikudayisi   Don't beat yourself up, we're brothers.

Yemi   Yeah, brothers.

Ikudayisi *exits.*

Yemi *picks up a basketball cap but then decides on the traditional hat. As he starts to put on his shoes he changes his mind and goes for his trainers. Once he has them on he stands in front of the mirror and checks himself out.*

Yemi   Yeah, I look heavy, man.

He begins singing and dancing around the room.

> Green white green on my chest,
> I'm proud to be a Nigerian!
> Green white green on my chest,
> I'm proud to be a Nigerian!
> Proud to be a Ni-ge-ri-an!
> Proud to be a Ni-ge-ri-an!